Naxalism

Causes and Cure

Attention Authors

Manas Publications is fighting a war to tell the world that India can win the battle not only by the bullet but also by pen. We are converting fighters into writers. There is no dearth of intellectuals in our country, however, their knowledge is confined to them only. No sincere effort has been made by any other publisher to channelise their knowledge, which is why the talent of every intellectual remains latent. An author always presents the raw material in the shape of a manuscript and it is the job of the publisher to convert it to a finished product. Manas has been continually motivating intellectuals and publishing their manuscripts for more than two decades and would like to publish your manuscript too. If you or your colleagues have a manuscript ready for publication or are working on it, contact us with a detailed synopsis and list of contents. Manas will also suggest you a suitable title for writing related to your area of expertise. Manas is known for its publishing quality. We take utmost care in publishing and also give wide publicity to the book and its author through our national and international distribution network.

Naxalism

Causes and Cure

Dr PK Agrawal, IAS

Additional Chief Secretary and
Commissioner General, Land Reforms
Government of West Bengal

Manas Publications

New Delhi-110002 (INDIA)

MANAS PUBLICATIONS
(Publishers, Distributors, Importers & Exporters)
4402/5-A, Ansari Road
(Opp. HDFC Bank)
Darya Ganj, New Delhi-110 002 (INDIA)
Off. ✆ 23260783, 23265523, Res. ✆ 23842660
Fax: 011-23272766
E-mail: manaspublications@vsnl.com
www.manaspublications.in

ISBN 978-81-7049-363-1
Rs. 595

Typeset at
Manas Publications

Printed in India at
Rajdhani Printers, Delhi
and published by Mrs Suman Lata for
Manas Publications, 4402/5-A, Ansari Road
(Opp. HDFC Bank),
Darya Ganj, New Delhi-110 002 (INDIA)

Dedicated

in the memory of my mentor
late Benoy Krishna Chowdhury
Ex Minister-In-Charge
Land and Land Reforms
Department and Panchayats
Government of West Bengal

[from 1977 to 1996]

Contents

Preface 9

1. Naxalite Movement: Origin and Growth 15
2. Land Reform Defined 25
3. Factors Constituting Land Reforms 35
4. Land Reforms: Law and Economics 43
5. Implementation of Land Reforms 49
6. Performance by various States and Union Territories under Land Reforms 69
7. Functioning of Naxalite Outfits 83
8. Strategy to Tackle Naxalism 91
9. Land Reforms in West Bengal 107
10. Distribution of Government Surplus Land in Uttar Pradesh 115
11. Land Reforms in Chhattisgarh 123
12. Land Reform Measures in Madhya Pradesh 129
13. Jharkhand: A Cradle of Naxalite Movement 137
14. Land Reforms in Bihar: Roadblocks 141

15. Protection of Land Rights of Tribals in Orissa 149

16. Land Reforms in Andhra Pradesh 157

17. Components of Land Reforms in Karnataka 173

18. Land Reforms in Maharashtra 183

19. Purchase and Distribution of Land 191

20. Streamlining Revenue Administration for Land Reforms 197

Index 207

Preface

Naxalite problem at present is India's gravest threat to internal security. To quote Prime Minister Manmohan Singh, 'not a day passes without an incident of Leftist extremism taking place at some place or the other'. Elaborating the alarming network of Naxalites, Ajit Doval, a former Director of the Intelligence Bureau (IB) had stated that Naxal activity affects approximately 40 per cent of the country's landmass and at least 35 per cent of the total population. The Naxal violence in states like Chhattisgarh, Jharkhand, Orissa, Andhra Pradesh and Bihar has been of late a regular affair. But what is worrying to the nation is penetration of its cadres deep into Maharashtra, Karnataka, Uttar Pradesh, West Bengal, Madhya Pradesh and other states including even UTs.

Where there is an injustice, violence is its natural fallout. If an equitable or egalitarian society is established in true sense, there will be peace. The equity can be achieved either by liberal releases of funds, goods and services by the State or by equitable redistribution of properties in the society. In rural India, most of the properties are locked in landed properties. Therefore, equitable distribution of land has been focussed or targetted since independence of the country.

The equitable distribution of land is the main demand of the Naxal outfits and this is the well pronounced policy of all successive governments as well. This is also the prime component of land reforms. Thus implementation of land reform measures can be termed as the solution for the Naxalite violence or movement in India.

The report of the expert group (EG) on "Development Issues to deal with the Causes of Discontent, Unrest and Extremism" associated with the Naxalite movement, set up by the Planning Commission in 2006, has in its report, 'Development Challenges in Extremism affected Areas', put forth the new approach that Naxalism is a political movement with a strong base among the landless and poor peasantry and adivasis, which, "in its day-to-day manifestation" is seen by its support base as "basically a fight for social justice, equality, protection and local development."

The National Land Reforms Council set up in October, 2007 under the chairmanship of the Prime Minister will also look into the issues of land reforms and will make specific recommendations on the policies relating to land, speedier disposal of land related cases pending in courts and quasi judicial fora i.e. revenue, courts etc., ceiling on land holdings, distribution of land to the eligible persons including the landless and homeless and for ensuring their possession of land. The problem of long pending court cases can be largely solved if 'Implementation of land reforms' is included as one of the Directives of the State Policy under Part IV of the Constitution of India. This will result in the various land reform Acts having overriding effect on fundamental rights and the rejection of bogus pleas of the landowners before the courts couched in beautiful language and phrases.

It is a wrong notion that land reforms have been accomplished in the country. Promulgation of an Act or statute *ipso facto* does not cure the disease it aims at. This is high time that the performance of various land related Acts or Regulations are thoroughly reassessed from objective and managerial points of view to achieve zamindari abolition, imposition of ceiling and other land reform measures. Even the fulfilment of objects of the Acts or statutes kept under the shield of Schedule IX of the Constitution should be assessed.

In fact, the United Nations in 1951 and in 1970 had declared that land reform is a continuous process and task. Even in Bible, it is spelt that after 7 times 7 years, a year of redemption follows, when all land goes back to the tiller without compensation to the moneylender or landlord. In all cases, it should be redistributed after fifty years. Originally land belonged to the community and it still belongs to the community. Engels (1878-1948) says that the issues of land property must be perceived in a dynamic way. If we take only redistribution of land, the distribution is never complete until each and everyone of the assignees of vested land gets possession and *patta* of the land allotted is given to him by the government. He must be made financially and socially capable to cultivate thc land. Any land lying fallow is an offence against the society or the State. Increase of productivity upto optimal level is also the ultimate goal of the land reform measures. Secondly, the correction and updation of land records or records-of-rights is also a continuous process. There are continuous changes in land scenario at the field level because of inheritance or succession, will, or partition among the co-shares or other written, oral or informal arrangements in the villages in vogue. These do not come before the land revenue or land reform officer for change or modification of records by way of mutations. Thus, there is constant need for the survey and settlement officials to visit the field to catch a glimpse of changed scenario in the field. The computerization of land records and setting up of common service centres at every gram panchayat level can help to know the latest status of land records or changes or modifications brought about as a result of registration of transfers of land that too if registration is integrated with revenue records. Thus, revision of land records is a continuous process like eight other components of land reforms. It is high time that sincere administrative attention is given to proper implementation of land reforms rather than brushing them aside in a casual fashion to shirk off responsibility as it is a mammoth task.

The protagonists of the Chinese model of liberalization and unprecedented progress should know that China has ventured in the field of liberalisation after distributing 90 per cent arable lands in between 1950 and 1980. More than 90 per cent landless households have received land in China. In India, these figures are around 5 per cent and less than 28 per cent respectively. Even in industrially developed Japan, 41 per cent arable land has been distributed and 81 per cent landless households have been given land. In Japan, agriculturists are given subsidy or incentives to cultivate land. The equitable distribution of land will ensure a peaceful foundation of the polity on which any industrialization or technological advancement can take off without any turmoil in future. In fact, in times of crisis in economy, agriculture sector through its production had saved India from collapse on many occasions. No country can depend on uncertain imports of foodgrains specially during crisis like war.

Thus, it is high time that land reform is recognized as the basic policy of India. This is also contained in Article 39 (b) and (c) of the Constitution of India. Adherence to land reform measures propelled by political and administrative will can solve many of the country's problems including the most serious problem of Naxalism looming large in the country.

This work has examined the age old concepts of land reforms in a new light. I know that any work on land reforms will be like a bubble in the vast country, yet a bubble has to be formed. The book has to be read as an integrated whole to tackle Naxalism through land reforms. Specific gaps in implementation of land reforms have been highlighted and solutions have been suggested. Repetition has been avoided. Accordingly, pending separation of Land Reform Acts between Bihar and Jharkhand, Madhya Pradesh and Chhattisgarh, the chapters on these states have to be read conjointly. Similarly, specific aspect of land reforms has been highlighted while dealing with different states. For instance in Bihar, aspect for gearing up the revenue machinery has been highlighted whereas in Madhya Pradesh, problems of tribals vis-a-vis forests have been elaborated. In Karnataka, the land tribunals have been dealt with in details so that one may know how pending court cases relating to land can be easily liquidated. In Maharashtra, need for institutional financing for assignees of vested lands and sharecroppers has been focussed specially in view of suicides by farmers in Vidarbha region of Maharashtra. In Orissa, the newly created serious problem of land acquisition in respect of marginal farmers has been analysed which has now emerged as an important segment of land reform. In Andhra Pradesh, the topic of land distribution has been analysed in all its practical aspects vis-a-vis demands of the Naxalites. In Uttar Pradesh, recording of share-croppers, *bataidar* or informal tenants has been taken up with detail. In West Bengal, ground level causes of upsurge of Naxalism have been brought out and how they have been practically tackled. Here, one new scheme in vogue is the distribution of small parcels of land known as "Scheme of cultivation, homestead and garden land" for the landless and this has been described in details where government purchases land and then settles with the landless beneficiaries up to 16 decimal so that there is no death due to starvation. Other state governments can emulate the scheme in suitable cases where no government land is available for distribution. Similarly, all other components of land reforms have been practically dealt with.

The topics have been presented in a simple and workable style so that appropriate land reform measures specific to the ground level situation to tackle Naxalism can be implemented in the field.

I am sure that this work will be helpful to the policymakers. It is a practical handbook to the administrators and officials of revenue as well as land reform departments who are entrusted with the task of land reforms at the field level in the country.

I thank Shri K Satyanarayana, IPS Ex-Superintendent of Police, Sonbhadra district UP who has enlightened me about the *modus operandi* of the Naxalites.

I express my gratitude to the Government of West Bengal for allowing me to publish this book.

PK Agrawal

1

Naxalite Movement:

Origin and Growth

The Naxalism is one of the major concerns in India. It is growing every day. Its historical analysis will help us substantially to understand about the problem and its solution. The 'Naxalism' is not a very old movement. It is sometimes termed as 'red terrorism'. It is very difficult to define age-old phenomenon like 'terrorism'. Schmid has tried to define 'terrorism' as follows:

"Terrorism is an anxiety – inspiring method of repeated violent action, employed by (semi-) clandestine individual, group or state actors for idiosyncratic, criminal or political reasons, whereby – in contrast to assassination – the direct targets of violence are not the main targets. The immediate human victims of violence are generally chosen randomly (targets of opportunity) or selectively (representative or symbolic targets) from a target population, and serve as massage generators. Threat and violence-based communication processes between terrorist (organization), (imperiled) victims, and main targets are used to manipulate the main target [audience(s)], turning it into a target of terror, a target of demands, or a target of attention, depending on whether intimidation, coercion, or propaganda is permanently sought[1]." No definition of Naxalism has been adopted so far. It is definitely not terrorism.

"Naxalite" word is derived from Naxalbari in Darjeeling District of West Bengal where there was a struggle in 1967 against the

---

[1] Alex P Schmid: *Political Terrorism - A Research Guide Book to Concepts, Theories, Data Base and Literature* (New Brunswick, NJ: Transaction Press 1983, p-70)

authorities with the avowed object of capturing power; Naxalites claim to be communist revolutionaries who swear by Mao Tse Tung's political thought; the movement started when CPI(M) leader decided to enter the Government after General Elections in 1967; revolutionary section resented it, for they thought violent revolution is the only way to capture power; Naxalbari, 6 km from Nepal, 22 km from Bangladesh, 120 km from Tibet, with thick forests and tribal population of 1,26,000 followed by forced seizure of land; another aim of movement was annihilation of class enemies, i.e., landlords, bureaucrats, etc. movement led by late Charu Mazumdar, Secretary General of Communist Party of India (Marxist-Leninist), CPI(ML), the political front of the party, as United Front Ministry was in power in West Bengal with CPI(ML) majority, Naxalbari movement launched on 3rd March, 1967, a number of people were killed, movement subsequently spread to other States like Assam, Bihar, Orissa, Jammu & Kashmir, Andhra Pradesh, Tamil Nadu, Uttar Pradesh, etc. the object was to bring armed revolution in the country[2]." The 'People's Daily', the mouthpiece of China Government supported the movement on July 5, 1967.

The Naxalites comprised of tribals, poor peasants, land labourers and students. By 1971, the movement spread to many districts in West Bengal but was crushed by the Congress Government headed by Siddhartha Shankar Ray ruthlessly causing a lot of violation of human rights.

The Naxalites also shrank and split within a brief span of 5 years due to fractional feuds and theoretical differences. However, the Naxals became active in Eastern Uttar Pradesh, Tamil Nadu, Bihar, North-eastern area of Andhra Pradesh, Kerala and Jammu & Kashmir. But their operation was rather weak in western Uttar Pradesh, Himachal Pradesh, Delhi, Punjab, Rajasthan, Gujarat, Maharashtra, Karnataka, Orissa, Assam, Manipur and Nagaland. In all the areas, where the economic condition of the people was better, the influence of the Maoist revolutions was

---

2. Chopra, PN, Chopra Prabh: *Encyclopaedia of India,* Agam Prakashan. Delhi, p. 277.

weak. Kanu Sanyal, who raised armed struggle through Peasants' Committee in Naxalbari during 1967 (March & April) to get recorded share cropper or bargadar was successful to some extent. However, after release from jail, he no longer professed violence during my meeting in 1993 as Director of Land Records and Surveys and Joint Land Reforms Commissioner reposed some faith in the administration. But he was critical about the non-allotment of Government vested lands and non-recording of bargadars in the area.

The legacy of Naxalbari was nonetheless real. It brought to the fore the political urgency of agrarian reforms in India which are popularly known as land reforms.

However, Naxalite movement found good takers in Bihar right from April, 1968 in Mushahari in Muzaffarpur district because injustice prevailing was writ large in Bihar. Scandal after scandal and the stink of corruption provided breeding ground for the Naxalite movement in Bihar and it soon spread its wings to contiguous districts of Rohtas, Singhbhum (now in Jharkhand), Gaya, Aurangabad, Bhojpur and Patna.

"There was gruesome massacre in Pipra which triggered off violence in Belchhi, where on May 27, 1977, Kurmis, a backward caste, killed 11 chamar (Harijans) in a land dispute which shook the conscience of the nation and late Smt. Indira Gandhi visited there. Similarly, one Harijan boy in Kanchi Kancherle in Andhra Pradesh was burnt alive for stealing brass utensils. Then followed a rash of violent incidents – in Kilavemani in Tamil Nadu where 25 Harijans were burnt alive in Villupuram; many areas of Marathwada following the Dalit Panther agitations caused a lot of ripples in Maharashtra."[3]

In Bihar, Yadavs are the biggest group. The hard working kurmis and koirees, mostly marginal farmers are the new contenders of power. Ammunition is freely available in the area and Naxalites all over get arms supplies from Bihar. In one single village 'Amaiya' in district Monghyr, there were 77 murders in one year.

---

[3] J.S. Tuman: *Communicating Terror*, Sage Publications, pages 13 & 14.

The police hobnobbed with landowners and lack of firm land records provided fuel to the fire. The Naxalites became active in tri-junction areas of Orissa, Andhra Pradesh and Madhya Pradesh (at present in the newly carved out State of Chhattisgarh) starting from the most neglected district of Bastar which found readymade support among the Indians. In Bastar, the tribals were not only poor without proper land entitlements, they were also exploited by the outsiders and were neglected by the local government officials. However, the Naxalites found easy shelter in bordering areas of two states that they can flee away after committing crimes like in trijunction areas of Jharkhand, Bihar and Orissa adjoining West Medinapur District of West Bengal. After the collapse of the Naxalite movement in Mushabari (Muzaffarpur), Srikakulan in Andhra Pradesh and the Wynand jungles in Kerala, the village Chauri in Bhojpur district of South West Bihar caught the media headlines on May 6, 1973.

"During 1982, the Indian People's Front (IPF) was launched in New Delhi at a national conference. In due course, IPF became the party's open political platform, actively intervening in national politics. Same year, the Third party Congress took place at Giridih, Bihar, where the issue of participation in elections was finalized. This shift in the outlook of CPI(ML) Liberation proved to be vital in designing the subsequent course of activity of the Naxal movement.

With this strategic shift in functioning, the CPI(ML) Liberation recorded its first electoral victory under the banner of the IPF in 1989 and Ara (a Lok Sabha Constituency in Central Bihar) sent the first "Naxalite" member to the Parliament. In a special conference convened in July 1990, the party decided to resume open functioning. This decision was formalized at its fifth Congress in December 1992. In 1994, the Indian People's Front was disbanded. The Election Commission recognized the party in 1995, and since then the CPI(ML) has been contesting successive elections at national and state levels.

PWG is the most important among all the splinter groups representing the Naxal movement because the dominant line within the Naxal politics today is the PWG line of thought. Though it is popularly known as PWG or PW, its official nomenclature is Communist Party of India – Marxist-Leninist (People's War). If today, Naxalism is considered as the greatest internal security problem and Naxals claim to be running parallel government in different parts of the country, its credit mostly goes to the PWG. The CPI(ML) (People's War) was formed on Lenin's birth anniversary on April 22, 1980. Kondapalli Seetharamaiah, one of the most influential Naxalite leaders from Andhra Pradesh and a member of the erstwhile Central Organizing Committee of the Communist Party of India, Marxist-Leninist (CPI-ML), is the founding father of the PWG; who later was ironically expelled from the group. On the other hand, with its parliamentary practices, Liberation was loosing its turf to PWG. Liberation, which once controlled the whole of central Bihar, was now loosing its territory and supporters to PWG and MCC. Not only in Bihar, but also elsewhere, Liberation was systematically shrinking on the map of Naxalite politics. By advocating electoral methods and not being able to make an impressive mark, the Liberation's way of movement became weak and the PWG's armed operations started gaining momentum.

So while the Liberation, with its changed modus operandi was being reduced to a small political party, the PWG in the same period, managed to register its presence outside Andhra Pradesh and gradually gained strongholds in different areas of Bihar, Orissa, Madhya Pradesh, Jharkhand, Chhattisgarh and Maharashtra. While the conflict between PU and Liberation made both groups suffer the loss of considerable numbers of their cadres; as already stated, it also resulted in the merger of PU and PWG and ultimately the violent consolidation of the movement.

Looking back, the need for a joint, unified platform was felt by the leadership of both the parties as early as 1981. The PW and MCC began unity talks from their very first meeting in 1981. However, the reason for the delay in the process was the lack of continuity of leadership. The arrest of Comrade Kondapally Seetaramaiah (KS), the leader of the PW, and later the internal crisis of the PW and split in the Central Committee (CC) delayed the unity process for several years. In the early eighties, the

MCC lost its two top leaders Comrades Amulya Sen (AS) and Kanhai Chatterjee (KC), which had some negative impact, resulting in further delay in the unity process."[4]

There are many Left Wing Extremist (LWE) groups operating in the country with a lot of underground and overground cadres and supporters.

While aiming to establish a classless society based on egalitarian principles and revolutionary struggles, resorting to violence remains the cornerstone of the major LWE groups. The CPM-People's War Group (53%) and Maoist Communist Centre (MCC) (30%) continue to spearhead LWE violence respectively.

The basic thrust of the different outfits is to focus attention on the grievances of the people, inequalities suffered by large segments of the population, release of victims of exploitation from the tentacles of the landlords, etc. and to inculcate 'class' responsibilities among the economically and socially deprived sections. In pursuance of these objectives, the groups have not only mobilized the people but have also ensured that distributive justice is available in a rough and ready manner. The peoples' courts organized by these groups expropriate surplus land from the landlords to be distributed to the landless, dispense criminal justice, settle disputes and punish offenders. Thus, 'Jan Adalats' constitute a cornerstone of their efforts to win over the masses, particularly in the rural areas. Besides, they indulge in extortion from businessmen, contractors, traders, government officers, etc., and resort to murders and kidnappings to eliminate interference by agents of the established administration and defiant class enemies.

Various LWE groups have their presence in different parts of the country, notably the heartland states including Andhra Pradesh, Bihar, Jharkhand, Madhya Pradesh, Chhattisgarh, Maharashtra, West Bengal, etc. The CPML-PWG is well entrenched in almost all districts of AP, several districts of central and south Bihar, Jharkhand, southern districts of MP, Chhattisgarh and Orissa and

---

4. Pandey, Sachchidanand: *Naxal Violence, A Social Political Study*, Chanakya Publications, New Delhi, page 69.

a few eastern districts of Maharashtra and three districts of West Bengal. The most afflicted districts have gone to the newly created state of Chhattisgarh. It also has a presence in a few districts of Karnataka and Tamilnadu.

The movement did not bring any immediate results in West Bengal and was short-lived but had far reaching implications and became a force behind numerous peasant struggles in different areas of West Bengal, Bihar, Jharkhand (by tribals), Chhattisgarh (by tribals), Andhra Pradesh and Punjab. However, the Left Front Government led by CPI(M) in its three successive terms starting from 1977 salvaged the situation by recording about fifteen lacs share-croppers known as bargadar under "Barga operation" programme. This was consolidated by proper distribution of surplus land. It is again following in West Bengal in 2009 after the implementation of land reforms has become secondary priority and development works specially by panchayat bodies have created more sense of discrimination on party lines rather than satisfaction.

Thus, Naxalism continued and resurfaced in Nineteen-nineties and onwards with more vigour and better organizational capability in other parts of India and is still continuing in full bloom. In India, Naxalite movement covers about 80 million landless people and 30 million tribals.

In the Naxalite areas, it appears that the Maoists are actually carrying out the reforms that the executive ought to have implemented, and are replacing the judiciary and the police in ensuring law and order for the poor and the oppressed. In Bihar, the government had taken under its possession land which had been declared as beyond the ceiling that a landlord can own. The government, the report states, "has the power to distribute such land to the poor, but has failed to do so". On the other hand, "the Naxalite movement has succeeded in helping the landless to occupy a substantial extent of government land whether or homesteads or for cultivation".[5]

---

5. Planning Commission of India: Report titled "Development Challenges in Extremist Affected Areas" by an Expert Group, EPW May 24-30, 2008, pages 11 & 12.

Similarly, in the forest areas of Andhra Pradesh, Chhattisgarh, the Vidarbha region of Maharashtra, Orissa and Jharkhand, the Naxalites have led the adivasis to occupy forest lands that they should have enjoyed in the normal course of things under their traditionally recognized rights, but which were denied by the government officials through forest settlement proceedings. While the government remained indifferent to the need for paying minimum wages to the adivasi tendu leaf gatherers in Andhra Pradesh, the Naxalites by launching a movement have secured increases in the rate of payment for the picking. The practice of forced labour ('begari') in the same state, under which the toiling castes had to provide free labour to the upper castes – and which should have been abolished by the government under Articles 14 to 17 of the Constitution – was done away with due to a "major upsurge led by the Naxalites in the late 1970s and early 1980s of the last century..."[6]

The government of Andhra Pradesh sat with the then People's War Group (now merged into Communist Party of India-Maoist) in October 2004, and agreed to a ceasefire till December 16 that year, and promised to consider in the meantime the Naxalites' main demand for distribution of land among the landless. But when the then Congress government failed to keep that promise, the Naxalites stepped in to forcibly distribute the land. The Government retaliated immediately by sending its police which gunned down Naxalite cadres in the forests of Warangal, West Godavari and other districts in January, 2005.

The Maoists may have to shelve their ultimate aim of seizure of power for the time being, and negotiate with the state in the humanitarian interest of the thousands of poor and innocent families who have been caught in the crossfire between the police and the Naxalites.

Thus, the basic cause of Naxalism is the glaring inequality in rural India based on unequal distribution of land and insecurity of tillers of lands to cultivate the land.

The Naxalite agitation subsequently found that inequality created due to developmental process can be more easily focussed

---

6. *Ibid*

to the have-nots. Secondly, they have to keep their cadres happy who have high expectations. Thirdly, they have to face onslaught of the police force. Hence, they have now taken up the cause of disparities in general prevailing in rural areas which result in favouritism shown by local officials, landlords and their political patrons in power and by panchayat representatives. This is appealing to the army of landless, hungry and poor dalits, and the tribals. But this cannot remain the focal point because the government can pour in enough money for development and use superior firepower to overpower them. At present, Naxalism seems to have been derailed from their main path of resistance movement. Therefore, it is essential for the Naxalism to keep land reforms in focus and the revenue administration in conjunction with general and police administration should try to implement land reforms with full sincerity and earnestness. Without people's support neither Naxalism survive nor can administration run smoothly.

2
Land Reform Defined

Land Reform can be defined as the redistribution of rights and interests in land in favour of the landless and the poor cultivators.

According to Shri SR Sankaran, "the term land reform encompasses the entire institutional framework of property relations or relations of production pertaining to land."[1]

Thus, land reform provides a means for redistribution of landed property through structural reforms which can bring about revolutionary improvements in the standard of life of the rural poor who have been deprived of their due rights in land due to domineering influence of the landed class in all spheres of rural life including political, administrative, social and religious.

Even if land reforms did not lead to effective redistribution of land in favour of the landless yet it has helped in bringing about a less skewed distribution amongst the landowners. The reforms had a favourable impact on the conditions of agricultural labour because of loosening of hold of monopoly in the rural economy in general.

As per a UN report in 1970, 7.5 per cent of households in India owned 59 per cent of the nation's land*. This skewed distribution of land resulted into social imbalances which surface in the form of social distortions like violence, suicide by farmers or rise in crimes in rural India.

---

[1] Yugandhar, B. N. (ed); *Land Reforms in India--Andhra Pradesh — People's Pressure and Administrative Innovation*, p. 17.

*In Mexico one per cent of the population owned 97 per cent of land whereas 96 per cent population has only one per cent of the land.

This results into absentee landownership. The zamindari systems of India and Pakistan provide notable examples. As a rule, zamindars and the middlemen neither did any agricultural work nor lived on their farms.

Ayub Khan, as dictator of Pakistan used the process of land reform in East Pakistan (now Bangladesh) to woo the middle class or big landlords as supporters and to act as instruments of his exploitative regime. According to him, "A Land Revenue Commission set up for East Pakistan in 1958 led to an amendment of the East Bengal State Acquisition and Tenancy Act (of) 1950, by which I was able to raise the ceiling of self-cultivated land from 33 acres to about 120 acres or so."[2]

The result is known to everybody. Pakistan was ultimately dismembered.

Recently constituted three new states in India i.e. Chhattisgarh from Madhya Pradesh, Jharkhand from Bihar and Uttarakhand from Uttar Pradesh have regions which were also neglected by their parent states from the point of view of land reforms.

In some of the countries in the Asian region, the extent of land redistributed up to 1970 was 43 per cent of agricultural land in China, 37 per cent in Taiwan, 32 per cent in South Korea and 33 per cent in Japan whereas in India, it resulted in redistribution of only 1.25 per cent of the operational area. China up to 1980 had distributed 90 per cent of her agricultural land.

In developing countries, the agricultural sector has the maximum weightage. In India it had been 46 per cent of GDP in 1960s (now less than 35%) and in Colombia, Pakistan and Philippines it had been 31 per cent, 50 per cent and 35 per cent respectively whereas in developed countries like Japan and America it had been 13 per cent and 4 per cent of GDP respectively.

Therefore, a 1970 UN resolution correctly says that this structural reform is an integrated programme with the aim to remove the barriers for economic and social development which follows from defects in agrarian structure.

National integration or communal harmony is the main problem of our country today. Land reform gives it the best and permanent solution.

---

[2] Ayub Khan, *Friends Not Masters*, p. 91

United Nation's Fourth Report says that "the redistribution of land can lead to the spread of national consciousness which is a precondition for a popular National Government. The greater awareness among farmers can lead to psychological integration. On the other hand, lack of land reforms, high mechanization, capital and intensive agriculture can cause agitation."[3]

Land reform measures aim at alleviating the rural poverty are as follows:

(1) Distributing land among the landless by taking over excess land from big landholders.

(2) Providing security of tenure and ownership rights to tenants and sharecroppers and by regulating rent payable by them to the landowner.

(3) Protecting tribal interests in land against alienation and encroachments by non-tribals.

(4) Consolidation of landholdings and thereby bringing about rearrangements of land for better productivity.

(5) Development of public lands for providing better access to the rural poor for fuel wood and fodder.

(6) Regulating usurious money lending and providing alternative sources of credit.

(7) Providing access to women to land and other productive assets.

(8) Protecting homestead rights of the rural poor on lands owned by them and providing them with house sites for construction of residential houses.

In India the landed property is the most important property because India lives in villages. Article 39(b) & (c) of the Constitution of India in the Chapter on Directive Principles of State Policy directs that the State shall ensure:

(b) that the ownership and control of the material resources of the community are so distributed as best to subserve the common good;

(c) that the operation of the economic system does not result in the concentration of wealth and means of production to the common detriment;

---

3. Agrawal, PK : *Land Reforms in India*, p. 56

It talks of proper distribution of landed property among the Indian citizens. There was obstruction in implementation of this directive earlier because article 31 & 31(A) relating to Fundamental Rights were in Part III of the Constitution of India relating to Fundamental Rights. Now the 'right to property' has been taken away from this Chapter and has been made only a constitutional right. In view of this, the Government can ensure egalitarian society through redistribution of landed properties.

"Economic growth without social justice is inhuman, but social justice without economic growth is impossible. And economic growth is equally impossible unless we combine the humanism of true socialism with the dynamism of private initiative which is loosely called capitalism."[4]

In India since the First Five-Year Plan, land reforms have remained a major issue of National Agenda for achieving agrarian reforms, for reconstruction of rural economy, ensuring social justice to "actual tillers" as well as landless rural poor and thus for creating sustainable base for overall growth of industrial and tertiary sector of our economy. The Central Government is playing an advisory and coordinating role in the field of land reforms as the subject is under exclusive legislative and administrative jurisdiction of the states as per Entry No. 18 of the List II (State List) of the VII Schedule of the Indian Constitution.

The major objectives of land reforms consist of re-ordering agrarian relations to achieve an egalitarian social structure, elimination of exploitation in land relations, realizing the age-old goal of "land to actual tiller", enlarging the land base of rural poor, increasing agricultural production, diversification of agricultural economy, etc. The major components of the strategy of land reforms are the abolition of zamindari and intermediary tenures, tenancy reforms, ceiling on ownership of agricultural holdings, distribution of Government wastelands including Bhoodan land, modernization and updating of land records system, special measures for prevention of alienation and restoration of alienated tribal land, improving empowerment of women to ensure greater access to land and abolishing gender bias in land legislations.

---

[4] Dr. Arnold Toynbee in *We, the People* by N.A. Palkhivala, p.73.

The Land Reform Acts contained in 9th Schedule of the Constitution enjoy protection of the Constitution. The objects of Land Reform Acts are:

(i) Abolition of intermediate interests, zamindaris, jagirs, inams;
(ii) putting a ceiling on the quantity of agricultural land to be held by a person, prevention of consolidation of holdings in excess of the prescribed ceiling, distribution of surplus land;
(iii) encouragement of co-operative societies to hold land other than individuals;
(iv) tenancy reforms for fixity of tenures, regulation of rents, conversion of tenants into owners; and
(v) preventing the fragmentation of holdings by prescribing a standard area below which no fragmentation will be allowed by transfer, partition or settlement.

In any land reform measure, the primacy goes to the redistribution of lands. It means and includes that the State should take over the surplus lands from the landholders in order to redistribute the same to the needy persons i.e. the tillers. Generally, the landless people constitute the poorest section of the rural areas. This is what a layman understands by land reform measure. All other measures support to achieve the right of cultivation for them. Under this category, second largest number of the landless or the land-hungry people are covered by recording them as sharecroppers, bataider, bhagidar or bargadar to assure them some sort of permanence in their right of cultivation. This is, therefore, given a second priority under land reform. Though this right does not mean transfer of ownership of land, yet the landowners become unnecessarily panicky. This right provides better security to the tenants just like the ad hoc or temporary government employees or workers in factories are given some sort of protection to continue in their jobs.

Historically, traditionally and conceptually, therefore, the following guidelines are suggested for better implementation of land reform measures:

1. The excess land should be taken over from the big landholders. The surplus land should be distributed expeditiously and should be accompanied by timely supply of inputs and investment support. J.R. Yojna/P.M. Rozgar Yojna or NREGP may be resorted to in order to assist the land reform beneficiaries. In areas not covered by such schemes, direct financing by the government will be necessary.
2. The ceiling laws should be amended according to the national guidelines based on the conclusions reached at the Chief Ministers Conferences on Ceilings of Agricultural Holdings in 1989 and should be included in the 9th Schedule of the Constitution.
3. Loopholes in existing laws should be plugged so as to secure complete tenurial and ownership rights on undertenants and sharecroppers.
4. Priority should be given to comprehensive programmes for preparation and maintenance of land records even where there is no statute for preparation of such records.
5. Special attention need be paid to tribal areas. Loopholes in laws applicable to tribals need be plugged and administrative machinery be strengthened. Cadastral survey of tribal areas should be completed where it has not already been done.
6. All tenants including sharecroppers should be identified, their right should be recorded and permanent heritable rights should be conferred on them before consolidation operations are started. In the programme for consolidation of holdings, land of small holders and surplus wastelands available for distribution should be consolidated in compact blocks to facilitate the future public or government investments for irrigation etc. to the underprivileged.
7. Publicity measures to be intensified to familiarize the beneficiaries and even the government servants charged with the implementation of land reform laws within the provisions of the law.
8. The administrative set-up be strengthened at different levels and should be imbued with direction and purpose.

9. Adequate plan allocation is required for financing of land reforms.
10. Associations or committees of beneficiaries should be established at village and block levels to fight for the rights of underprivileged and to advise on implementation of all measures of land reforms and provision of supporting facilities to beneficiaries. Landless and sharecroppers and small landholders should be adequately represented on these committees.

At the field level, the following points can form the basis to work out factors of land reforms in a generalized way:

1. Distribution of government wasteland and implementation of Bhoodan Act, where such legislations exist.
2. To detect benami lands; to analyse about lands under court's injunction and to gradually reduce the limit of land ceiling to accommodate the less poor.
3. Granting permanent rights of homestead to landless/homeless persons and implementation of homestead tenancy legislation where such law exists.
4. Removal of encroachment on government lands and redistribution of such lands to landless persons. Restoration of land alienated by the tribals in contravention of the law, in tribal areas.
5. The definition of personal cultivation should lay stress on the following ingredients : (*a*) The person claiming to be in cultivation of the land must bear the entire cost of cultivation; (*b*) He must cultivate his own land by his own labour or by the labour of any member of his family; (*c*) He or member of his family should reside for the greater part of the year in the locality where the land is located; and (*d*) Cultivation should be the main source of his income.
6. No transfer of agricultural lands should be permitted to be made to any non-agriculturist.
7. The tenants (whether occupancy or non-occupancy) dispossessed by force or by fraud or by any other illegal means from their land must be restored to their possession as expeditiously as possible.

8. The field data has shown that there are large number of sharecroppers/tenants at will, who have been working with the same landowner for a number of years and are entitled to be conferred the status of occupancy tenant/owner within their respective states. All such tenants should be conferred with the status of occupancy tenant/owner with retrospective effect. Even those who have been evicted or shifted from earlier plots should be restored to the status of occupancy tenant/ownership right. The recognized Kisan Sabha/Peasant Organization/Voluntary Organization/Activist Organization should be associated in such effort and their evidence on the tenancy status of an incumbent should be made admissible.
9. If the landowner does not give receipt to the non-occupying tenant, the sharecropper should be allowed to deposit share of the produce of landowner with the nearest authority. The landowner should be made liable to criminal prosecution for refusal to grant receipts. Onus of proof should be shifted to the landowner to establish that the latter is not cultivating the land.
10. The tenants in the cultivable lands of religious institutions, trusts, mutts, etc., should also be conferred with ownership right in respect of these lands. These institutions may be provided with annuity.
11. Resumption of land by landowners from tenants for self-cultivation should not be allowed except in case of physically-handicapped or serving army personnel.
12. Ejection of tenants for non-payment of rent should be prohibited.
13. The small and marginal farmers who are compelled to lease out to big landowners should be linked with institutional agencies, anti-poverty programmes and rural development schemes (like Jawahar Rojgar Yojna/ P.M. Rozgar Yojna, ITDP*, etc.) to make their farms viable. If they lack implements, irrigation facility and inputs, such facilities should be extended to them.

---

*ITDP stands for Integrated Tribal Development Programme

14. In case of a dispute between the landowner and the persons claiming to be tenants/sharecroppers, the onus of proof should be on the landowner to prove the negative.
15. Sharecroppers should be legally included as tenants within the tenancy reform laws.
16. Special drives should be launched to identify informal tenants/sharecroppers in all the states who should be immediately conferred occupancy tenant/ownership status. In this drive, the local Peasant Organizations/Agricultural Labour Organizations/Voluntary Organizations/Kisan Sabhas and other activist groups should be actively associated.
17. Inadequacies in the administrative organisation should be removed. It should be land reform oriented.
18. The recognized local Peasant Organization/Agricultural Labour Organization/ Voluntary Organization/Activist Organization should be permitted to file claims for the conferment of occupancy right/ownership right to sharecropper/non-occupancy tenant before the appropriate authority.
19. Cooperative farming should be encouraged in villages on the pattern of Egypt. Panchayats may be nodal agencies to organize these. Arrangement for marketing, implementation and servicing should be available at Panchayat.
20. General awareness and conscientization camps should be organized in every state having pockets of high tenancy.
21. Implementation of legislation relating to moneylending and abolition of moneylending.
22. Updating and maintenance of land records in a computerized form and implementation of legislation if any, enacted therewith.
23. Political will should be created. For this, landless, small and marginal farmers' representatives should be given place in local panchayat bodies and ministries so that they are associated at each decision-making level.
24. Emphasis should be given to social reforms so that the farmers enjoy the benefits of reforms as healthy contributors to society.

25. Panchayats should be organized and be really independent in their affairs. They should be associated with implementing land reforms measures. They may be given power to dispose of petty land matters and development of farmlands also.
26. The poor peasants may be provided legal aid up to the level of the Supreme Court. The various stages of land litigation should be reduced. Land tribunals may be set up to reduce the pendency at the High Courts as substitutes for speedy disposal of cases. The Lok Adalats should be empowered to dispose of land reforms litigations along with prompt disposal of cases by rural courts i.e. Nyaya Panchayat/Gram Nyayalayas.

3
Factors Constituting Land Reforms

The following factors can be considered to arrive at a mathematical formula for quantifying land reform. The following linear equation has been suggested.

The term factor analysis embraces a variety of techniques. Our discussion focuses on the one procedure 'principal component analysis' and the factors derived from the analysis are expressed as linear equations. These linear equations are of the form:

$$T(LR) = R_1L_1 + R_2L_2 + R_3L_3 + R_4L_4 + R_5L_5 + R_6L_6 + R_7L_7 + R_8L_8 + R_9L_9 + R_{10}L_{10} + ... + R_nL_n$$

T(LR) is the Total/Resultant Land Reform.

R is the weightage or ranking of the factor.

L indicates factor related to land reform on the basis of conclusions arrived at earlier. It may represent one factor or combination of factors. The factors are thus as follows:

L_1: Existence or implementation of Employment Generating Schemes like Jawahar Rojgar Yojna, NREP* ITDP or IRDP** or PM Rojgar Yojna or NREGP.

L_2: Whether tenancy or sharecroppers are recorded or unrecorded and are given their rights. They should not be ejected.

L_3: Practice of cooperative farming or assistance by Panchayats by developing local leadership and helping the cultivators locally in all matters.

---

*NREP stands for National Rural Employment Programme.

**IRDP means Integrated Rural Development Programme.

L_4: Distribution of government surplus land after vesting in State and giving possession to the pattadars or assignees of the vested lands after distribution of surplus lands and thereafter.

L_5: Position of land records, detection of benami lands and whether land has been equitably distributed and passbooks of land-details have been issued.

L_6: Extent of social and religious reforms.

L_7: Availability of legal aid to the landless agricultural labourers, pattadars, sharecroppers or poor peasants.

L_8: Financial assistance or credit for supply of timely inputs and other investment support.

L_9: Success of consolidation operation.

L_{10}: Allotment of house sites and restoration of alienated tribal land or lands transferred due to distress.

The above equation can thus be represented as:

$T_{j(LR)} = R_i \; L_i$ And R_i is the multiplication factor of where $i = 1,2,3,4,......10......n$

The co-efficient R_i may be determined for each factor depending on the relative importance of that factors. R_1 R_2 R_3 R_4 R_5 R_6 $R_7 R_8$ R_9 R_{10} or any other co-efficient or factor taken later on.

The weightage *inter se* can bc determined by developing closed-ended response based on the concept or decision of the research. Here, one cannot avoid subjectivity. To reduce the subjectivity, even detailed discussion can be made to determine the allocation of the weightage. For this purpose, a rating scale may be fixed. Rating scales, by and large, try to secure the intensity of the respondent's feelings on a pre-defined sets of response alternatives. Here, guidance has been taken from Likert Scale which is also called a 'summated ratings' scale. Let us construct the following six statements or decisions relating to issues under investigation, very adequate, adequate, so so, inadequate, very inadequate, nil. Let us assign the numerical values oı rank ranging from 0 to 10 different categories as follows:

very adequate	assigned	10 marks
adequate	assigned	8 marks
so so	assigned	4 marks

inadequate	assigned	2 marks
very inadequate	assigned	1 mark
nil	assigned	0 mark

Using this method of scoring, total scoring is calculated depending on the strength of the factor.

Let us, therefore, assign percentage importance to each factor taking clues from discussion in Chapter 1 of this book.

T(LR) is taken as 100 per cent. Therefore, each factor will be determined on the basis of 'a'/100 where 'a' represents percentage weightage *inter se* of each factor. L_1: 4 per cent is given maximum value for Employment Generating Schemes during lean season of work or otherwise. This can be maximum as R_1L_1 = 10* .04 = .4

L_2: 20 per cent weightage is given to recording of sharecroppers and protection to their rights of cultivation. Therefore, L2 factor will be 20 per cent in ideal condition but on-rating scale, it will vary from zero to 10* .2 = 2

L_3: Local assistance, it is given 10 per cent weightage. If the Panchayats are established and are functioning well, there is semblance of cooperative farming or pisciculture and there are organizations of pattadars, agricultural labourers or sharecroppers, the adequate weightage will be given. In case of ideal situation of covering the entire village through cooperative farming, full weightage or very adequate category will be given. However, before the stage of cooperative farming, rural organizations are necessary to safeguard rights of cultivators.

L_4: 40 per cent weightage is earmarked for distribution of government vested lands. This is the main target specially in the Indian context. In fact, aim of imposition of Ceiling Acts is to take away excess lands from the big landholders and to affect redistribution. It is not sufficient that the lands have gone to government but also should be distributed. Therefore, if the lands are still with the local landlords, it will be of very inadequate category. If the lands are vested to government but possession is not taken over, and benami lands are not unearthed, it will be within inadequate category. If the Acts have been implemented, this will be 50-50 category of case. If the lands are distributed but the possession is not given, it will be classified as adequate category. Only in case of lands properly allotted alongwith possession given over, it will be classified as 'very adequate' category allocating 10 marks.

L_5: Weightage eight per cent is given to the position of land records and existing position of landownership or landholding. If lands are more or less equitably distributed and there is no cultivation beyond ceiling limit in the village, it will get allocation of rank within 50-50 category. If land records along with village maps properly do exist, then it will have a ranking in adequate category and if passbooks detailing individual holdings are distributed, it will be a perfect system in 'very adequate' ranking with full 10 marks.

L_6: Total weightage three per cent is given to social and religious reforms. Poor people spend a lot of money on festivals and ceremonies and do not go for work for a number of days just to celebrate many unknown local festivals or rituals due to superstition or orthodoxy. They also indulge in indebtedness and drinking. If there is lot of indebtedness, it will be 50-50 or normal category or average category. Social reform like keeping villagers away from gambling or drinking, will earn "adequate classification". If the agriculturists are free from religious dogmas, they will be placed in the highest ranking.

L_7: Weightage three per cent is allocated for legal aid to the .poor. If legal aid is available only through mutual conciliation without any statutory system, it will fall in very inadequate ranking. If conciliation or disposal of disputes are done through the aegis of Panchayat bodies or Nyaya Panchayats or official agencies, it will fall within inadequate category. If legal aid facilities are available up to revenue courts, it will be in 50-50 or normal category. If legal aid is available up to district judge court's level, it will be adequate. And if legal aid system free of cost actually is available up to High Court, Supreme Court level, it will be given the highest ranking.

L_8: Five per cent weightage is given for financial assistance for crops through government or cooperative or Panchayat agencies including subsidies. This also reflects the credit facilities available for cultivation to delink the sharecropper or pattadar from the moneylender. In this category, mostly crop-credit finances are included, i.e., credit available to purchase plough, cattle, manures and seeds etc. However, if soil conservation work has been done or irrigational facilities are available, the village will be placed in very inadequate or inadequate rankings respectively. If credits from banks are available, it will be of adequate category. If government subsidies are available fully, then the situation will be of very adequate nature.

L_9: Only one per cent weightage is given to consolidation operations. Without co-operative farming consolidation has come under criticism due to corrupt practices. Therefore, if the consolidation operations are started, it will be of 50-50 category. If the *chaks* or plots are finally demarcated, it will be of adequate category. If the plots are dispute free, it will be placed in 'very adequate' ranking.

L_{10}: Six per cent significance or strength is given equally to allotment of house sites to the rural poor as three per cent and three per cent for restoration of alienated land due to distress. As tribal population is very scanty, the restoration of tribal land has also been put in the latter category. If the house sites are allotted, it will be adequate ranking. If the house sites are so made that the poor classes are free from fear of the upper classes, and they are properly put in effective possession, the ranking will be very adequate. In ideal case R_{10} is ten.

In case of ideal situation, all R_{js} will have 10 ranking points. Accordingly, the estimate may be made whether a village, subdivision, district or state comes within the type of category i.e., very inadequate, adequate, 50-50, inadequate or very inadequate state of affairs of land reforms.

The coefficients in the factor equations are called *"factor loadings"*. They appear in each factor column, corresponding to each variable. The equation may be depicted in a random case as

$$R_{(LR)} = 10L_1 + 8L_2 + 0L_3 + 0L_4 + 4L_5 + 0L_6 + 0L_7 + 2L_8 + 1L_9 + 1L_{10}$$ where L_1 ... to L_{10} are fixed already.

The factor loadings depict their relative importance of each variable with respect to a particular factor. In the above equation, we have got positive loading factor indicating that they are variables of importance in determining the extent of land reform in a given sample. Similarly, some factors with negative attribute may be included which pull back land reforms. But as this study is a part of legal study, there is not much scope to go into minute details. It is to concretize the ideas so that real focus may not be lost sight of while viewing the land reforms as an integrated whole.

The above equation is reduced in number form as follows: $T_{(LR)}$ = I0*0.04 + 8* .2 + 0* .1 + 0* 4 + 2* + .08 + 4*.03 + 0*.03 + 0*03 + 2*.03 + 0*.01 + 2*0 = .4 + 1.6 + .16 + .12 + 0 + 0 + .06 + 0 + 0 = 2.34 which is in inadequate category.

It means that the important factors to contribute for land reforms are distribution of surplus land, recording of sharecroppers and organizing the rural folk for implementation of land reforms. The three factors will amount to 70 per cent of resultant land reform i.e. $T_{(LR)}$.

In the ideal solution, the factors derived will explain 100 per cent of the variance in each of the original variables or factors.

There are two important subjective issues which should be properly resolved before employing factor analysis model.

1. How best the factors should be employed in attempting to reduce the data? How best the criteria should be used in establishing that number?
2. The labelling of the factors is intuitive and subjective.

The following resultant land reform (LR) is obtained for the State of Uttar Pradesh.

$T_{(LR)}$* = .003 (I) + .2 (II) + .1 (III) + 1.6 (IV) + .32 (V) + .03 (VI) + 00 (VII) + .1 (VIII) + .4 (IX) +.48 (X) = 3.23 i.e. about 32.3 per cent.

---

* stands for Employment Generating Scheme
II stands for Position of Sharecroppers
III stands for Cooperative Farming
IV stands for Distribution of Surplus Land
V stands for Status of Land Records
VI stands for Social and Religious Reforms
VII stands for Availability of Legal Aid
VIII stands for financial assistance for crops.
IX for consolidation and
X for allotment of house sites

Applying preceding empirical formula, we find that land reform over 50 per cent category should be good. Beyond 80 per cent, it should be adequate. On the basis of above formula we find extent of land reform in two states of India is as follows: i.e. U.P. and West Bengal, 32 per cent and 67 per cent respectively.

Similarly, the formula can be successfully applied to assess total land reforms from macro to the micro level i.e. from national level to state, district, sub-divisional/taluka/tahsil, block or village level and accordingly, corrective steps can be taken to improve the extent of land reform at that level.

In West Bengal we may give following weightage:

L_1 = As landless and poor farmers get only about 15 days work out of 150 days required. The work is allotted more or less equitable except little party colouring which should not be there. Poor is poor irrespective of caste, creed, community, colour or political affiliation.

Therefore, weightage will be just below average, i.e. inadequate = 2.

L_2 = This factor of recording of sharecroppers is very successful. Though as per an estimate there are more sharecroppers and there can be conferment of ownership rights to them like in Maharashtra. Yet this factor gets full marks due to very poor performance of other states in this regard. Therefore R_2= 10.

L_3 = This factor also gets good marking as Panchayats and Krishak Organizations are very strong so much so there is hardly any scope of injustice to the poor farmers unless contrary takes place. Moreover, as cooperative farming is yet far off and efforts by governmental agencies are nil, this may get adequate marking, i.e. eight.

L_4 = There is equitable distribution of land more or less but all lands could not be distributed yet as about 1.70 lakh acres of land is locked in litigation. Therefore, this factor can only get at the most adequate category, i.e., 8.

L_5 = Position of land records is as backward as any other state. There is no provision of regular updating. However, by induction of lowest level functionaries, i.e., revenue inspectors at the Gram Panchayat levels, the situation is likely to improve. Therefore, it is averaged R= 5.

L_6 = Social and religious factors are little dormant in society but are very much effective in personal lives. Therefore, farmers are occupied with the rites and rituals. L_6 is therefore, very inadequate with 1 rating. Neither Panchayats nor religious reformers are active in this field.

$L_7 = R_7$ = 5 because there is not much availability of legal aid to the poor in West Bengal.

L_8 = Facility of crop credit is satisfactory through Panchayats but due to poor recovery, bankers retard progress. It will be of average category, i.e.R_8=5. Allotment of house site is OK but construction is inadequate.

L_9 = Neither consolidation is taken up nor is likely to be taken up. Therefore R_9=0.

L_{10} = Restoration of alienation land due to distress is done but restoration of land to tribals shows lethargy as cases before special officer, scheduled castes and scheduled tribes are not processed expeditiously. The factor gets a weightage as adequate = 8.

*Calculating above factors, we find

T(LR)= .4 x 2 (I) + 2 x 10 (II) +.1 x 8 (III) + 4 x 8 (IV) + .8 x 5 (V) +.3 x 1 (VI) + .3x5 (VII) + .5 x 5 (VIII) + 0 x 1 (IX) + .6 x 8 (X) = .8 + 20 + .8 + 32 + 4 + .3 + 1.5 + 2.5 + 0 + 4.8 = 66.7% = 67%.

*Which is over 50 per cent category but is below adequate category (80 per cent).

4

Land Reforms:

Law and Economics

Land reforms are basically redistributive measures of landed properties. India has about 70 per cent of rural population.

The share of agriculture in GDP of India is as follows :

1950-60	49.4 per cent
1990-00	27.7 per cent
2001-02	22.5 per cent

Purchasing power in rural India should improve to increase GDP.

2. Constitutional Background

The Constitution (First) Amendment Act, 1952 added two new articles 31A and 31B and added the Ninth Schedule to the Constitution. Land reforms aim at protecting 'Right to Property' of greater segment of population. One of the directives of the State policy under article 39(b) reads that 'the ownership and control of the material resources of the community are so distributed as to subserve the common good'.

In Golaknath case, the Supreme Court held that the amendment cannot be made by Parliament so as to take away or abridge the fundamental rights enshrined therein including right to property. The concept of property right in Part IV is conditioned by social interests and social justice.

State List Entry 18 of the Constitution reads as : "Land that is to say right in or over land tenures, including the relation of landlord and tenant and the collection of rents, transfers and alienation of agriculture land, land improvement and agriculture loans, colonization. Article 31(1) has been reenacted in the form of article 300-A by the Constitution (Forty Fourth Amendment) Act 1978. Now remedy is available by a civil suit, or statutory remedy, if any, say by way of damages and not under Article 32 or 226.

Land reform measures involve joint efforts by the states and the Union.

3. Cases pending in Courts[1]

Table I

Cases and area in litigation in High Courts

(Implementation of Land Ceiling Laws)

State/UT	High Court	
	Cases	Area in acres
Andhra Pradesh	1254	44424
Assam	61	23596
Bihar	648	50098
Karnataka	1165	94402
Kerala	1501	27657
Madhya Pradesh	271	21232
Rajasthan	201	21800
Uttar Pradesh	2060	40496
Total	**7161**	**323705**

Thus, the High Courts can dispose of number of pending cases involving lakhs of acres of surplus government land by constituting specialized benches.

[1] Quarterly Progress Report (cumulative) on implementation of Land Ceiling Laws for the quarter ending December, 2000, published by department of land resources, ministry of rural development and department of justice, ministry of law and justice, Government of India.

Ceiling limits in various states[2]

Actual ceiling limits in various states (Area in ha)[2]

State	Irrigated with one crop
Andhra Pradesh	6.07 to 10.93
Bihar	10.12
Gujarat	6.07 to 19.73
Haryana	10.90
Karnataka	10.12
M.P	10.93
Punjab	11.00
Rajasthan	10.93
Tamilnadu	12.14
U.P	10.95
West Bengal	5.00

* 1 ha = 2.42 acres = 11712.859 sq.yards

Personal Cultivation

The apex court consistently upheld the practice of personal cultivation.

Resumption of land by the landlord

The Supreme Court cautioned the High Court not to go into the merits of the case but decide questions of facts (not before it) in its writ jurisdiction.

[2] Agrawal, PK : *Actual ceiling limits in various states, Land Reforms in India*, M D Publication, New Delhi, p.198.

Land held by deity to continue as Debuttar

Many religious and social organisations are exploiting the government and indeed the poor by availing exemption from ceiling limit, which land would otherwise go to the downtrodden landless farmers.

Tenancy Reforms

Tenancy reforms more or less depend on quality of drafting of legislation. Publicity of tenancy movements by tenants like bargadars certainly affect the minds of courts favourably as judges do not work in vacuum.

The Government of Maharashtra is turning the clock back by acquiring lands of many landless in the Konkan division.

Ceiling on Land Holdings

The Supreme Court devised means to evade ceiling by planting the trees on surplus land.

Bar to Civil Jurisdiction

The Supreme Court agrees that the jurisdiction of civil courts stands ousted in matters where revenue courts are empowered to grant relief yet many civil courts continue to entertain matters under the garb of title suit or appeal from a judicial court will only be in a higher judicial forum.

Records of Rights

The R-o-Rs produced through computers can claim presumption until they are challenged.

Allotment of Surplus Land

The Apex Court is inclined to support the protagonists that the larger plots are more beneficial for productivity though this concept has now been exploded. The doctrine 'small is beautiful' is equally applicable in the land sector.

Land Reforms and Productivity

It is a bogy spread by the vested interest that fragmentation of lands result into less mechanism and less investment in agricultural sector. The measures of land reforms contribute to the higher productivity in land due to the following reasons :

(1) Human Resource Development (HRD)

(2) All economics matrix/calculations take into consideration the cost of human labour while arriving at the cost of production. In old age, when a person is unable to do any hard labour, he at least can grow some vegetables, forest or cash-crops without feeling useless in life.

In fact experiments by two major NGOs in Gujarat and Maharashtra and by Rural Development Institute, USA, have proved beyond doubt that even small patches of land have been instrumental to increase production by way of harvesting water and joint agricultural operations supported by government schemes, cooperative credits, mutual cooperation and joint efforts. Implementation of land reforms has definitely resulted into higher productivity in a few states as in West Bengal.

Advantages

The higher productivity due to land reform has two pronged advantages :

a. The assignees of the vested lands or the sharecroppers can make farming cooperative societies without disturbing the individual ownership on the Egypt pattern.

b. The diversion of middle class youths to their lands will reduce unemployment and law and order problems in rural India.

Indifference to Land Reforms

The first and the foremost reason is that the present administrative or political elite is deft in the art of fire fighting. Secondly, the political elite don't want to work hard. The public also believe in 'personality cult'.

It is in this context that even sometimes the socialists have regarded land reforms measures as opium for masses as they delay the onset of blood-revolution.

An Ideal Concept

FAO of late, has supported the concept of small farms.

According to FAO, "redistribution of only five per cent of farm land in India, coupled with improved access to water, could reduce rural poverty levels by 30 per cent under what they would otherwise be, so that in Indian conditions of land and water reforms would be a key approach." Thus, the process of land reform is required to be hastened in India. The solid base of land reforms will provide a strong platform to the economy to take off. Both are complementary to each other.

5
Implementation of Land Reforms

The innovation is about the methodology of implementation of land reform measures. The need for implementation of land reforms has been accepted by one and all. The doubt and curiosity is how these measures can be successfully implemented. Land reform as a solution to extremists' agitations in various states has by and large been agreed upon.

I was associated with the implementation of land reforms in West Bengal from day one of the Left Front Rule in West Bengal since 1977 as an IAS officer.

I have projected in my book 'Land Reforms in India' how the land reform measures can be successfully replicated in the largest State of India i.e. UP without any change in laws relating to land in UP.

In this Chapter, I have lucidly stated how the twin measures of land reforms i.e. recording of sharecroppers and distribution of surplus government lands were implemented in West Bengal so that these could be easily replicated. To simplify the procedure, more emphasis is laid on practical experience rather than on academic or semantic discussions.

I am sure that some of the public conscious energetic and dutiful bureacrats and politician will take some clues and implement the land reforms in their own way in the changed circumstances.

Introduction

Land reform basically is the redistribution of rights and interests in land in favour of the landless and the poor cultivators. In this chapter only two major land reforms innovations are being dealt with which were actually undertaken in West Bengal.

Every political party promises to implement land reform measures before elections but few of them take it seriously after they win the elections. But it was an exception after the landslide victory of the Left Front parties in West Bengal in 1977 led by the Communist Party of India, Marxists (CPI-M). The Left Front allies had come to power with a specific mandate to implement land reforms. I was one of the presiding officers in this election. After the Left Front came to power, they reorganized the State apparatus for this purpose and gave it first priority in their governance. They were lucky that their predecessor government had passed requisite pro-land reform legislations. The only need was to implement them in the field. The previous government had made about seven hectares as maximum permissible land to be held by any raiyat/ person. In addition, they had provided under section 16 of the WBLR Act 1955 that anybody cultivating land of another person on condition to deliver a share will get 75 per cent share of produce if the person who cultivates the land, known as bargadar, provides plough, seeds, cattle, fertilizers, irrigation and other inputs.

Operation Barga

Without waiting for administrative arrangements for implementation of the above provisions, relating to the tenancy cultivation/barga cultivation, the Krishak Sabha, peasants' wing of CPI(M), started harvesting crops of landowners in an organized manner and removed the produce to their place (khamar) for separation of grains. Earlier these harvested crops used to be taken to the central place controlled by the landlord or the landowner where he used to control the process of separation of produce and then he used to distribute the share of the bargadars at his sweet discretion. The landowners in such cases, never allowed more than 50 per cent of produce after harvesting, to the sharecropper or bargadars. The sharecroppers started claiming 75 per cent of produce, where there were dispute with the landowners or the relations between the landowners and the sharecroppers were strained. In few cases, disputes arose when the exploited sharecroppers or local peasants' organizations wanted to settle some score with the landowner, who enjoyed uninhibited power in the village so far. The administration stood by the side of the sharecroppers as per the changed political scenario. As a result, the landowners approached the local administration like block development officer (BDO) and junior land reform officer (JLRO) now known as block land & land reforms officer (BLLRO). The BDO was authorized to mediate between the two in the presence of the local peasants' organizations on behalf of the sharecropper. The peasants' organizations took a tough and uncompromising stand in most of the cases with their earlier experience of rough behaviour by landowners with them. Now law and administration both were on their side. Earlier landowners could exploit them by keeping the administration specially police administration on their side. However, the administration slowly veered around the sharecroppers and poor cultivators in the villages and started the process to get the sharecroppers/bargadars to be recorded. In the process, many unscrupulous bargadars under the umbrella of the peasants' organizations also took undue advantage and started cultivating land and harvesting crops for which they had no right. It was essential to show the cultivation through sharecropper as the landowners did not cultivate land personally. He cultivated through him and there was an agreement to allow him to cultivate his land. This agreement in the village is to be inferred through conduct because village economy runs mainly paperless and cashless. Therefore, if the alleged bargadars had been cultivating land of the landowner peacefully for the past two/three years, he was presumed to be bargadars unless otherwise it was contradicted. Or the landowner could show that he cultivated through daily labourers and that he maintained lists of those daily labourers and the proof of payment of their due daily wages. The landowners in rural West Bengal never gave receipt for produce he got from the bargadars nor maintained a register for cultivation through daily labourers. The peasants' organizations took advantages of these legal lacuna and slowly they controlled the cultivation scene in rural Bengal. I used to settle such harvesting disputes as BDO which were questioned by the Commissioner as regards their legal basis. Seeing one sided swing in the rural area, which led to law and order and legal problems, the local administration approached the policymakers unanimously to get bargadars recorded. This is what the political elite at the state level wanted. Without creation of demand for amendment of rule or law, the rule or law is not implemented in spirit and with speed. The top bureaucrats headed by Shri D Bandyopadhyay, IAS with the requisite will, drafted a programme for barga, recording throughout the state. Operation Barga accordingly as a programme, was launched in West Bengal on 5th July, 1978. As per report before 1977, the total number of bargadars recorded was: 154,816 (CS)* + 30,681(RS)** = 1,85,497.

As per estimate of peasants, organizations, there were 7,47,716 bargadars, whereas as per census there were about 6,86,188 bargadars in the State. Therefore it required special attention. Apart from this, the then minister-in-charge of land and land reforms department Shri Binoy Krishna Chaudhury declared in the West Bengal Legislative Assembly on 13th March, 1978 that recovery of benami lands will be a priority of the state government. These lands after identification will be vested in the state and thereafter, in due course distributed among the landless persons as per the well laid down norms which are more or less the same all over the country. With these twin objectives in place, the new Left Front Government in West Bengal started its journey towards social engineering and formation of an egalitarian society in rural West Bengal. I was associated in Operation Barga as Subdivisional Officer, Barasat where VIPs used to come to see the new methodology from its beginning.

The legal provisions were strengthened by amending Rule 21 and schedule A of the West Bengal Land Reforms Rules, 1955. The schedule A was amended by amending the second proviso by providing that the settlement officer could direct "that names of bargadars shall be incorporated in the record-of-rights by the revenue officer subordinate to him after holding such enquiry and after giving the persons claiming as bargadars and the owners of the land concerned such opportunity of being heard as the revenue officer may deem fit". On the question whether individual notice or general notice should be given for the purpose of giving opportunity of being heard,

---

*CS stands for cadastral survey.

**RS stands for revisional survey.

the relevant rule was amended in 1981 [proviso 2 was added to CL.1 of Schedule A appended to W.B. L.R. Rules, 1965]. It was now laid down that opportunity of being heard would be deemed to have been given if within one week before the enquiry, the revenue officer publishes a notice of his intention of enquiry by fixing a notice at a conspicuous place in the office of the Gram Panchayat concerned. Two "Explanations" were further added, thereby legalizing the issue of bargadars' certificates. The second amendment closely followed, and the revenue officer was authorized to incorporate in the record-of-rights changes on account of barga cultivation by making necessary enquiries. These amendments accorded the required legal sanction to the methodology of Operation Barga. The immediate impact of Operation Barga was encouraging, as was reflected in the budget speech of the minister. It was indeed a matter of satisfaction to note that the rate of recording accelerated by 357 per cent compared to the rate of RS recording, within a span of 6 months from July to December 1978. The table below gives the figures in detail:

Table 5.1: Recording of Bargadars up to 31.1.1979[1]

Name of District	Numbers of Bargadars
1	2
Bankura	40,709
Birbhum	32,749
Burdwan	36,805
Coochbehar	35,405
Darjeeling	7,870
Hooghly	42,433
Howrah	23,187
Jalpaiguri	31,777
Malda	46,421
Midnapore	88,678
Murshidabad	31,614
Nadia	24,439
Purulia	—
24 Pargana	75,443
West Dinajpur	55,164

As Operation Barga gained momentum a counter-propaganda by the land owners, and sometimes their counter-move, was discernible in the media and in the courts of law. This was not unexpected, as a reaction to attempts at structural changes. One of the criticisms was that adequate notice was not given to the land owners though the existing system of giving notice was legalized by an amendment of the West Bengal Land Reforms Rules 1965. According to this amendment, parties interested would be deemed to have been given an opportunity of being heard if the revenue officer published a notice of his intention to make an enquiry for recording names of bargadars by affixing the notice at a conspicuous place or by beat of drums. This amendment was followed by another in which granting of a barga certificate under section 50 of the West Bengal Land Reforms Act 1955 was legalized. Originally, Operation Barga was to be completed by 30th June, 1979. The Board of Revenue extended the date to 31st December, 1979. An assessment of the result showed downward trend in the rate of recording of bargadars. While extending the date of Operation Barga to 30th June, 1980, the Board of Revenue issued a departmental circular in which it was stated that while there was no need to change the methodology of Operation Barga, there was a great deal of need for the officials to follow the standard procedure with more sincerity. As a result of further drive, by 30th April, 1980, 8,54,740 bargadars were recorded, as compared to 5,72,694 bargadars recorded by 31st January, 1979. The monthly average recording in this period was 18,803.

The programme of Operation Barga was further extended first by two months – to 31st August 1980, and then again by three months, to 30th November 1980. Total number of bargadars recorded by August 1980 was about 9.5 lakhs. Thus, in two years' time names of about 4.5 lakhs bargadars were recorded under the crash programme of the Operation Barga continued and upto September 1987, 13,75,284 bargadars were recorded. Later on the addition per year was gradually declining. As on date i.e. up to October, 2007[2], 15,10,173 number of bargadars have been recorded covering a area of 1,11.12,71 acres.

Further assuming that in the present set-up and legal framework, 25 per cent of the bargadars will remain outside the records. Thus, we may reasonably conclude that the total number of bargadars in West Bengal will be around 20 lakhs[3]. On the other hand, the excess vested land in the State would be around 15 lakh acres.

Salient Features of the 'Operation Barga'

The entire State of West Bengal (except areas of Purulia district and Islampur subdivision which were ceded from Bihar), was for the purpose of this scheme, divided into two areas : (a) Area 'A' consisting of about 24,000 mouzas already covered by Khanapuri Bujharat (KB) and (b) Area 'B' comprising the remaining 18,000 mouzas not covered by KB. For the purpose of hastening the process of recording the names of bargadars, it was decided that in Area 'B', a crash programme called 'Operation Barga' was to be undertaken to cover the entire area within one year i.e. 30th June 1979. Priority pockets with large concentration of bargadars would have to be selected in consultation with peasants' organizations and composite squads of officers consisting of junior land reforms officers and kanungos would have to cover the specified priority pockets within a very short time. In respect of Area 'A', 'Operation Barga' would be taken up in a selective basis on information received on joint or individual petitions or from other sources.

The methodology was : A squad will, after giving due notice, hold an evening meeting on the first day at a venue which is a place of habitual congregation of bargadars and agricultural labourers. A group of mouzas may be taken at a time and a general public notice will be given. Care will be taken that these four points are cearly discussed in the meeting : (a) legal and economic benefits that will accrue to recorded bargadars (b) security of the right of cultivation, (c) pooling of funds flowing of like FFW, ITDP, NREP, IRDP, etc.[4] Similar programmes are still there with changed nomenclatures, and (d) need for a supportive organization of their own for the enduring benefits of land reforms. During and after the meeting, names of bargadars will be tentatively enlisted. On the next day, field enquiry and verification will be made and the verified list will be displayed at a public place so that objections if any could be raised. On the third day after hearing objections, if any, names of bargadars will be recorded and bargadars, certificates will be distributed. In this way, names of bargadars would be speedily recorded within the four walls of West Bengal Land Reforms Act 1955 and the Rules framed thereunder. This is the programme of 'Operation Barga'.

Vesting and Distribution of Government surplus land

Up to 1977, 11,22,000 acres of land were vested to the State. Out of that, only 6,12,000 acres of land were distributed among the landless poor. There were three problems in this area of land reform;

Firstly, the beneficiaries who were given government surplus land (known as assignees of the vested lands or pattadars), were not put in possession of land. Some of the land continued with the erstwhile owners or their agents.

Secondly, the assignees of the vested lands or pattadars, were arbitrarily selected because the local member of the legislative assembly (MLA) indirectly controlled the selection process of beneficiaries. He had no time and his representative indulged in all sorts of malpractices with the connivance of the local land revenue wing of the Collector of the District.

Thirdly, lot of land was still lying outside the net of vesting as these lands belonged to influential persons of ruling political party mainly Congress or to other local influential persons including so-called charitable organizations or to big money lenders or strong Zamindars.

First problem was solved easily as the CPI(M) had their own wing of *amins* or land experts who were conversant with those lands. They with the help of block level land reforms officials then known as junior land reforms officer (JLRO) put these persons in real possession with the help of their peasants' organizations. The landowners could not procure assistance of block level administration or the police as they were scared of strong backlash by the ruling party.

As regards the second problem, self contained circulars were issued for preparation of lists of beneficiaries. By that time, panchayat bodies also came into existence. It was laid down that all lists of beneficiaries or pattadars will be processed through the *sthayee* or subcommittee on land reform of the Panchayat Samity (block level panchayat body). This provided double check and also provided scope to activate the land reform machinery for this work. The priority in distribution was given to the persons in possession of land. Under Section 49 of the WBLR Act, the preference in settlement of government land shall be given to the persons belonging to scheduled tribe and then to the scheduled caste. No person holding 1 acre (0.4047 Ha) land will be entitled for government land. He will have to personally cultivate the land and land was not made transferable. However, sometimes while considering priorities, political favourtism was shown by the panchayat subcommittee pressurizing lower level land reform officers.

To tackle the third problem, efforts were made to unearth benami lands kept by the erstwhile landlords in the names of their agents, dogs, animals or other distant relatives or friends. The test was as to who was enjoying the usufructs from the lands. The WB Land Reforms Act further restricted the exemption only for the public, religious and charitable trusts. It imposed a family ceiling and the ceiling remained more or less around 25 acres. Exemption for tank fisheries, orchard and private forests were also taken away. All lands were made at par. Thus, possibility under garb or disguised classifications was done away with. This gave all the impetus to track down benami lands, bring them under ceiling net and then distribute among the landless poor cultivators.

Methodology adopted

The distribution of government vested land was also taken up in the drive mode. It was decided to organize patta distribution camps or patta distribution programmes which was attended by a state or district VIP. In this camp, beneficiaries will be brought to a block level venue where some pattas will be distributed from the stage. Then, rest of pattas will be distributed through counters like in the election. The pattadars will be given advice that they should preserve the patta/lease documents with safety and security like their own mother as land is mother. They should not mortgage this land whatsoever adverse situation they may come across. Transfer of patta land in any form including mortgaging is prohibited by law. Thirdly, they should cultivate land themselves or through members of their family. In some of the camps, bankers were invited to provide credit to the new assignees of the vested land at a minimal rate of interest of about four per cent. This was essential because once a bargadar or pattadar is recorded in government records, his traditional link with the village landowner is cut off and usual flow of credit to him is barred. This gave a lot of momentum to the land distribution programme. The land reforms functionaries also worked hard day and night and prepared patta documents which otherwise were neglected due to other routine works in the block level/taluka level revenue offices. This work was also accomplished in a drive mode. It is unfortunate to mention that the administration at all levels in the country has lost their focus on their mission. They get indulged into day to day affairs so much, mainly in court cases and employees' matters that the main work programme becomes the last priority. Therefore, the main work of the land reform office was to be done through the camp or special drive so that under the fear of VIP visit, the surplus land could be distributed. The villagers benefited from the programme as they were transported either by the panchayat functionaries or by the land revenue functionaries to the venue and were given land document. At some places, they were also given the copy of record of rights/r-o-rs, known as parcha in West Bengal or khatauni in other parts of India and had not to pay any extra money to receive land. The programmes were extensively covered by the Press and TV channels. That created competition among district heads to come in limelight. The VIPs like the Land Reforms Commissioner could also satisfy themselves on the spot that the lands were being distributed to the deserving persons and they were actually handed over the pattas for the land.

During the camp, the local land reforms functionaries were clearly instructed to hand over possession of land for which documents were distributed. Thus, they could not take any plea subsequently. In West Bengal, the villagers under the panchayats and peasants' organizations are quite conscious and vigilant and they ensured that possession of lands were handed over to them. This way, the possessions of lands were restored to the old and new pattaholders in rural areas.

I successfully implemented this programme during my five years tenure as Addl. District Magistrate (Land Reforms) in districts of Purulia (1980-84) and Murshidabad (1985-86) and carried it further as District Magistrate and Collector of Coochbehar District (1986-1987). I also distributed land identity cards personally signed by me to all tribal pattadars and most of the scheduled caste pattadars in these three districts making an innovation at the district level which was subsequently approved by the State headquarters. Then, as the Director of Land Records and Surveys, (1992-93), I organized various patta distribution camps attended by the then minister-in-charge, land and land reforms late B.K. Chaudhury who was next to the chief minister in status in the Government of West Bengal. I repeated the same thing since I took over as Principal Secretary and Land Reforms Commissioner of the department of land and land reforms and I found to my utter surprise contrary to general expectation, that all lands have not been distributed. In fact, I find government surplus land in continuous flow like the flow of a stream. The lands are otherwise kept under cover by the local land revenue or land reform machinery because distribution of land always creates ripples in the otherwise peaceful set-up of the officer or the village. In West Bengal alone, 1.8 lakh acres of land is beyond the reach of the landless peasantry because the courts have yet to decide whether these lands will go to the State or to the landowners. The dumb majority of the landless persons does not find its spokesmen easily and they leave their situation to the fate. If the land is given to them, this is the dearest and the best. They certainly bless the officials as well as politicians who arrange land documents to them for life. Their loyalty is not wavering like the loyalty of the Indian middle class which changes after every five years. Therefore, everybody should participate in the 'yajna' for the good of the society.

Benefits from 'Operation Barga'

In the first place, the very name "Operation Barga" has become a familiar term all over the country. It has become synonymous with recording of tenancy rights of cultivators. The bargadar cultivators on the one hand feel secured of their tenure of cultivation which will not depend on whims and fancies of the landowners. On the other side, the landowners immediately felt a sense of deprivation that they will lose their land once names of bargadars were recorded. Slowly and gradually both reconciled and have accepted a situation where both will coexist side by side. Both are happy as production has since considerably increased because land is cultivated by the actual tiller who has permanent right of cultivation which is heritable. Therefore, on the whole the landowner continues to get at least that share which they were getting before 'Operation Barga'. But it is surprising that under pressure from the political elite, no bargadar has been terminated for not giving proper share or getting the land cultivated by another person through informal letting out. This should not happen. But in the field of land reforms, developments are guided to a certain extent by political will apart from the administrative whims and statutory requirements.

The price of land with bargadar has gone down considerably because the bargadar cannot be generally evicted. The widows and old men suffer most because they cannot till their own land and their land cannot be sold at an economic price as no purchaser would like encumbrance of a bargadar. Thus, they fear to lose their land and livelihood. But in rural areas, the families are still joint and these incidents are stray. The landowners have organized themselves under the banner of Bhumijivi Sangh and are trying to stall these measures even up to the Supreme Court. The Operation Barga is not an end in itself. It is a means to an end to carve out a secure existence for the bargadars in the hostile social environment in the interest of public good. This public good is achieved in two ways. Growth and prosperity depend on peaceful situation, and most of the cases of breach of the peace in the countryside have their genesis in land disputes. Unrecorded bargadars are always prone to eviction and insecurity and form the subjectmatter of a law and order problem. Secondly, optimal food production of the country has a direct causal relationship with security of land tenure, no matter whether the parcel of the land is an economic holding or not. Recent researches have proved that on the whole, the rate of food crop production is size-neutral to the holding and that on the contrary, motivation and security being equal, unit production rate by the owner of a smaller holding is generally greater and more efficient than by the affluent owner of a large holding having even the advantages of mechanized farming. In a labour-intensive economy like ours, with little capital-formation, ensuring social security and motivation to the actual tiller can undisputedly hasten growth. Operation Barga, by hastening the process of barga-recording, is likely to hasten the pace of security and motivation of the bargadars. According to a Chinese proverb, more number of times a cultivator visits his farm, more is production.

The Operation Barga has also provided security of tenure to the Left Front Government to some extent in West Bengal who have been ruling the State for the last thirty years. This has proved to be a good impetus to other political parties to implement land reform measures in their own states who otherwise were not coming forward even to listen about land reforms measures, let alone the implementation. The main target of all political parties is how to win election. Now a days, a lobby of neo-liberalization of economy has been advocating against sharecropping system as the real estate companies or entrepreneurs cannot purchase or acquire land for making housing and malls without compromising with bargadars, at a higher price for the land by way of arranging additional premium to the bargadars on land. This has not been accepted by the Left Front Government who are generally against real estate boom as it does not generate adequate employment. There is no objection if real estate companies give jobs to bargadars after eviction. However, they are averse to employ them even during construction stage.

There is a suggestion to create a State Land Corporation and Regional Land Corporations for bargadars where the Corporation will advance credit for purchase of lands intended to be sold by the sharecroppers[5] which will be recovered in easy instalments. If bargadar does not agree to purchase, the Land Corporation will purchase on grounds of need or distress of the landowners, and settle with pattadars. In the changed scenario, reverse tenancy has started. Even small cultivators have started leasing out their land due to lack of credit facilities and inputs. This is a wrong tendency. Fear of recording sharecroppers can check this practice. If it is not done immediately the rural India will become very unstable and violence may erupt now and then. Insecure and uncertain individuals are potential source of violence and resultant instability in the society.

It will be agreed by all that mere recording of bargadars' names will not guarantee them security and motivation. A whole basket of measures are necessary to free them from the clutches of their exploiters who sometimes appear to them to be benevolent. Liquidation of rural indebtedness, provision of alternative sources of input and maintenance finance, protection from legal persecutions, effective implementation of the lawful rights of the bargadars, provision of social security by way of old age pension, etc., implementing minimum needs programmes, State programmes for effective organization of bargadars and many similar measures will be the meaningful package deal for the benefit of bargadars.

Distribution of Government vested land

Before drive for distribution of government surplus land was undertaken, the total lands distributed was 6,12,000 acres to 9,63,000 beneficiaries. The same figure in October 2007 stood 11,18,341 acres to about 29,54,749 (Oct-2007)[7]. It means that about 1 crore population was benefited by this innovation by creating 20 lakh additional pattadars.

Area of vested agricultural land increased from 11,22,000 acres to 13,12,227 (Oct. 2007). Thus, the main impact was due to drive to distribute the land not by way of vesting through unearthing benami lands. There is a limit to the availability of land as it cannot be stretched like rubber. This included 10,96,600 scheduled caste pattadars and 5,32,857 scheduled tribe pattadars. This exposes governments like UP and Bihar who are projecting themselves as champions for schedule castes but are not making basic impact on the living of scheduled castes in rural areas.

Similarly, it is an eye opening to separatist agitation or extremists' agaitations for the cause of scheduled tribe pockets of North Eastern States, Darjeeling, MP, Chhattisgarh, Andhra Pradesh, Bihar, Jharkhand and Orissa. The Naxalite agitations get diluted because of this basic work done by the administration in West Bengal after 1977 as a drive and with the full support and the strong political will of the ruling parties.

The wide gap between land legislation and its implementation was plugged to a large extent. It was ensured that the pattadars were given possession of their lands which were well protected by the local peasants' organizations. Institutional financing from banks and cooperative societies was also arranged so that these pattadars could develop their land and contribute to the increase in production of foodgrains in the State. It really happened in practice. The State which earlier used to be a food-deficit became a food surplus State and started exporting foodgrains like rice, potatoes to other states. This has been accepted by all governments. The former chief minister of Orissa Biju Patnaik[8] unequivocally accepted that the increase of productivity in West Bengal was due to extensive land reform measures and he ordered for their replication in Orissa. But before he could gear up his party and administration for the purpose, he died. Now, further innovations are added to this drive. The name of wife appears as first beneficiary on patta document so that the male pattadars may not mortgage or transfer patta land due to debt, drinking habit, gambling, etc. Secondly, self-help groups are being formed so that they may get credit from banks and purchase high cost equipments like tractors, harvesters, etc., centrally and also arrange for the marketing of products centrally. Thus, cooperative farming is being promoted keeping the individual ownership intact. This will ensure entry of West Bengal in a new era of agriculture production and marketing without exploitation by intermediaries at the second stage of land reforms. The ultimate purpose of land reform measures is to increase the production of foodgrains in the country. The panchayat bodies, have enthusiastically come forward to assist the pattadars and bargadars through various labour generating schemes and through rural housing and rural sanitation schemes like the Indira Avas Yojna. As panchayats are dominated by the real leaders of the village folk, they care for their fellow poor people. Even few bargadars and pattadars head local gram panchayats. Many are members as such. Thus, it is not the lip service but actual administrative structure which helps the poorest of the poor in West Bengal.

As the quantum of land left is not much for distribution, it is being distributed in small parcels so that a person can make his home and do some vegetable cultivation on adjoining area along with rearing his cattle. This, at least will ensure, that he will not die due to starvation. Under the Acquisition of Homestead for Agricultural Labourers Act 1975, 3.18 lakh beneficiaries have been given pattas for homestead purpose. An innovative scheme[9] is under implementation in West Bengal where the land is purchased and distributed to the BPL landless persons up to 15 decimal to construct their homestead and for garden cultivation. This is most essential in areas where land is no longer left for distribution but there is a huge demand for land from the poorest of the poor section of the society.

Thus, if we take total beneficiaries, wider the land reform measures in West Bengal, these 48 lakhs are covering about 2.4 crore population out of 9.25 crore (approx.) population of the State at present. This is the population which is satisfied and forms the bedrock of peace and tranquility in the village from where the State can take off for any development including industrial development to cater specially for the urban poor.

Replication in other States

There is no problem in replication of these innovations by adopting these types of procedural strategies within the existing framework of law and rules prevailing in every state. It has been shown that in UP[10] similar Operation Barga for recording of sharecroppers or bataidars or bhagdar can be undertaken within the framework of the UP Land Revenue Act as amended by the UP Land Laws (Amendment Act 1977). The land reform laws of Orissa and Bihar have similar provisions. Similarly, an Operation Barga type drive was undertaken in Kerala and it was successful. States of

Andhra Pradesh, Bihar and Jharkhand are sincerely looking for such options in near future.

In Northern India, there is a large presence of informal tenancies (not less than 11 per cent) and similar operation, can be undertaken easily. In Maharashtra,[11] and Tamilnadu the system is for conferment of ownership to the tenants. However, it might be difficult in North Eastern States, where lands belong to the community and land laws are different.

As far as vesting of excess land from the landowners is concerned, the Benami Transactions (Prohibition) Act 1987, a Government of India statute can be applied in all the states. So far only 60.27 lakh acres of lands[12] have vested to states which should be at least double of that. The State laws are otherwise competent enough to unearth and recover benami excess lands from the clutches of landowners. The distribution of government vested land requires drive on the pattern of West Bengal which can be easily followed because it is only a procedural change which has made the difference. For undertaking distribution of government vested land, a technically sound machinery will be required which can measure and demarcate the land promptly. Secondly, number of revenue staff and officials will be required to be increased alongwith imparting them training. In West Bengal, the Department of Land and Land Reforms is a major Department of the Government having about 30,000 employees. IAS officers having top reputation are posted in the department. The Department is held in high esteem by all other departments and political executive. This can be easily done in other states. In other states, at present, the department of revenue is neglected and ignored. Its power is further diluted by setting up of the board of revenue with more senior officers than the principal secretary. If board of revenue is entrusted with land reform measures then they should also be accountable before the state assembly. Power and accountability should go side by side. In West Bengal, board of revenue no longer exists. Attempts are to be made to impart training to the revenue staff and officials in computerization of land records so that records of rights[13] are fed in computers including maps which can be continuously updated with each transfer of land or change in plot size or boundary which is being done in West Bengal as a second phase of land reforms. Moreover, West Bengal has yet to integrate its land records with the registration department like Andhra Pradesh and Karnataka so that the records of lands can be continuously updated.

Factors contributing to the success

Main factors contributing to the success of land reform measures in West Bengal are;

(1) The peasants/cultivators are well organized under the umbrella of various strong and powerful peasants' organizations like Krishak Sabha, Samjukta Kishan Sabha, Agragami Krishak Sabha which are under political parties CPI(M), CPI, RSPI, FBI and others in their respective pockets of influence.

(2) The new and young administrators are trained and motivated to get themselves involved in the land reform works by the political executives in a friendly environment and thus, a group of IAS officers are well groomed and motivated in this field who can be regarded as experts in the field. Their expertise is further passed on through training and interactions with the lower level functionaries.

(3) The Government of West Bengal attaches top most importance to the department of land and land reforms and directorate, land records and surveys and tries to assist and support them in all ways. They try to give them maximum allocation of funds and personnel within the budget constraint. Such is the will of the Government in West Bengal to implement land reforms. The officers and officials in the department are not transferred or victimized at the instance of landowners or powerful persons whose lands are to be subjected to cultivation by the sharecroppers or are to be vested being excess beyond the prescribed ceiling limit as per relevant law.

After farmers' agitations in Singur and Nandigram in West Bengal, recent long march of Tribals of Vidarbha from Central

India to the Capital New Delhi, incidents of suicides by farmers in Vidarbha (Maharashtra) and Andhra Pradesh and Naxalite agitations in Andhra Pradesh, MP, Chhattisgarh, Bihar, Jharkhand, Orissa, all governments have woken up to pay due attention to the rightful causes of farmers, sharecroppers, cultivators and the landless. None can dispute if poor tribals parade to the Capital of the country to demand land for them which is their basic necessity. None should deny the right of cultivation to the villagers if their lands are acquired for industrial or commercial purposes to accommodate requirement of new liberalized era to take India into the 21st century. An appropriate and due rehabilitation package has to be devised for them preserving their right of cultivation. A villager is not generally fit or an expert to do any other thing except cultivation. How can one deny this basic right of life and livelihood to him? If this great army of disgruntled landless persons and poor cultivators is not given their due rights, it will run over the prosperity created by the neo-liberalized era of economic activities in the country.

Karl Marx has termed land reform measures as anti-revolution as these delay blood revolution. To avoid bloodshed land reforms be implemented with all sincerity and earnestness. It will help to create a peaceful and stable society in India ready to take up any challenge in coming times towards development and progress.

References

[1] Source : *Land Reforms in West Bengal — A Statistical Report* compiled by the Government of West Bengal. 1979, Land & Land Reforms, Writers' Buildings Secretariat, Kolkata – 700001.

[2] Source, *Monthly Progress Report for the month of October, 2007* published by Director of Land Records & Surveys, WB, Survey Building, 35, Gopal Nagar Road, Alipur, Kolkata-700027.

[3] Ghosh, T.K. *Operation Barga & Land Reforms.* P-99.

[4] Food For Work Programme, Integrated Tribal Development Programme. National Rural Employment Programme, Integrated Rural Development Programme.

[5] As per Section 21C. WBLR Act. 1955

[6] Left Front Government in West Bengal. Page 14. I&CA, Deptt. Govt. of West Bengal, Writers Buildings, Secretariat, Kolkata.

[7] *Monthly Progress Return of Land Revenue Works,* Director of Land Records & Surveys, WB. Pages 9, 11, 12.

[8] *Land Reforms in India,* (PKA), page 206.

[9] The scheme is known as "scheme for donation of land for homestead and cultivation" (Chas-Basobaser Bhumi dan Prakalpa) and is in vogue since 2005-06 in West Bengal with initial provision of Rs. 30 crore.

[10] *Land Reforms in India,* (PKA) pages 146-147.

[11] In Maharashtra, 1.492 million tenants were declared owners of land on 2.512 million hectares. But they had to pay price of land which was between 20 and 200 times, the annual land tax. About 30 million tenants got ownership rights. Of which 66 per cent got without any payment. As per an estimate there are 15 million concealed tenants.

[12] *Annual Report 2006-07,* Ministry of Rural Development, Govt, of India.

[13] Other land reform measures are employment generating schemes, development of peasants' organizations, social and religious reforms, legal aid to the poor peasants, credit for cultivation, consolidation and allotment of house sites, ref: Issues in Land Reforms.

6

Performance by various States and Union Territories Under Land Reforms

Successful reform of land tenure in densely populated states, as in Kerala and West Bengal, leads to a slow change of rural social relations and power structure, but does not overcome other socio-economic problems, like unemployment and under-employment. The legalistic approach, observance of all jurisdical procedures, compensation payments, etc. slow down the pace of change and diminish the re-distributive effect, thus it also limits the new investment in the farming sector."[1]

West Bengal is the leader in the field of land reforms for the following reasons:

(1) Intermediary tenures have been done away within agricultural and non-agricultural land.

(2) About 15 lakh sharecroppers known as bargadars have been recorded and their rights of cultivation are heritable.

(3) The ceiling in West Bengal is five hectares for irrigated area and seven hectares for non-irrigated areas inclusive of both agricultural and non-agricultural land.

(4) Land in possession of small and marginal farmers is 60 per cent in place of 29 per cent which is the national average.

(5) Land Tribunal has been constituted.

(6) Over 3.5 lakh persons have been given homestead instead of land.

---

1. Bergmann, Theodor : *Agrarian Reforms in India,* Agricole Publishing Academy, p. 192.

(7) Tenantwise records of rights are being planned and computerization is being introduced.

(8) The percentage of land owning cultivators has increased to 41.9 in 1981 from 31.2 per cent in 1971.

Performance in other States

In Karnataka, occupancy rights are conferred on dwelling houses, constructed by agricultural labourers on lands belonging to others. Land tribunals have 4 non-official members, out of which one shall be from S.C./S.T. community. Lands held by institutions are brought under the ambit of the Act.

Gujarat has done fairly well in the field of land reforms because of its sound administrative base through active Panchayat System. The following steps have been successfully taken:

(1) Occupancy rights have been conferred on the inferior holders or permanent tenants numbering about 12.41 lakhs including tenants.

(2) Absentee ownership has been effectively eliminated by the provision requiring personal cultivation.

(3) The records are regularly rewritten after 10 years.

(4) As recommended by the Government of India, the Ceiling Act 1974 was amended in 1974 to provide a maximum ceiling of 10 to 18 acres of perennially irrigated land and 30 to 54 acres of dry crop land.

(5) Allottees of surplus land get financial assistance of Rs. 2,500 per hectare which is treated as subsidy under the centrally sponsored scheme.

(6) Land held by the scheduled tribe will not be transferred without the prior permission of the collector.

The achievements under land reform measures are encouraging in Tamil Nadu. There are about 4,94,000 registered tenants cultivating lands belonging to individuals and Public Trusts to an extent of about 6,85,500 acres. The Government is also seeking the cooperation of social workers in the rural areas for proper implementation of the land reform laws. Finally, steps to reorient the attitudes of the revenue and police officials in the matter of protection of the rights of the rural poor vis-a-vis the landed rich have been effectively taken.

In Maharashtra, by 1970, ownership of leased land was partly or fully transferred to the tenants in about 18.75 lakh tenancy cases, out of a total of about 26 lakh recorded tenancy cases in the State. The ceilings were lowered in 1975, as a consequence of which an area of 1,60,962 ha was declared as surplus. Out of the total area of 2,85,455 ha declared as surplus under these enactments, 2,51,522 ha have already been distributed.

State of Madhya Pradesh is a leader in the maintenance of land records. There is a mechanism for continuous updating of records of rights and maps. The individuals have also been provided with their up to date land details in the form of passbooks.

In Assam, the ceiling in rural areas has been fixed at 6.68 ha per family while in urban areas the ceiling is 2000 sq. meters per family. Recently, in March 1990, the government has made penal provisions for violations regarding purchase of tribal lands.

In Andhra Pradesh, voluntary declaration of concealed land by the landowners will save them from the punitive actions provided in the Act. In Andhra, the tenancies were based traditionally on oral contract and those too, have now been recorded and thus established the tenants rights and legitimacy.

The smaller states showed the following characteristics:

In Jammu & Kashmir, under Agrarian Reforms Act 1976, the rights in a holding of land of any person not cultivating it personally, were extinguished and vested in the state.

In Orissa, Raiyati rights have been conferred on more than 1.6 lakh temporary lessees. In Tripura, civil court's jurisdiction has been barred.

In Goa, where the tenants are cultivating on communidade (community) land, they have been so recorded in the land records. In Sikkim, there are effective provisions to ensure that there is no arbitrary termination of cultivation. In Puducherry, the right of resumption for personal cultivation was withdrawn totally except for the armed forces personnel. In Manipur, the Revenue Tribunal is dealing with cases under the Manipur L.R. & Land Reforms Act 1960 in place of conventional judicial courts. In Meghalaya, there is community ownership of land and land cannot be acquired even for public purposes without scrutiny by people's representatives and community. In Mizoram, the government is deeply concerned with the non-productive development of land by the allottees and also allotment and transfer of land to non-agriculturists.

Computerisation of Land Records (CLR)

The centrally sponsored scheme on computerisation of land records (CLR) was started in 1988-89 with 100 per cent financial assistance as a pilot project in eight districts viz; Rangareddy (AP), Sonitpur (Assam), Singhbhum (Bihar), Gandhinagar (Gujarat), Morena (MP), Wardha (Maharashtra), Mayurbhanj (Orissa) and Dungarpur (Rajasthan) to remove the problems inherent in the manual systems of maintenance and updating of land records and to meet the requirements of various groups of users. It was decided that efforts should be made to computerise core data contained in land records, to assist development planning and to make records accessible to people/planners and administrators.

The main objectives of the scheme are:

1. Ensuring that landowners get computerized copies of ownership, crop and tenancy and updated copies of records of rights (RoRs) on demand.
2. Realizing low-cost and easily-reproducible basic land record data through reliable and durable preservation of old records.
3. Ensuring accuracy, transparency and speedy dispute resolution.
4. Facilitating fast and efficient retrieval of information for decision making.
5. According legal sanctity to computer-generated certificates of land records after authentication by the authorized revenue official.
6. Setting up a comprehensive land information system for better land-based planning and utilization of land resources.
7. Focusing on citizen-centric services related to land and revenue information.

Under the CLR scheme, financial assistance is provided to states and UTs for completing data entry work, setting up computer centres at the tehsil or taluk or block or circle level, subdivisional level, district level and a monitoring cell at the State level. Funds are also provided for imparting training on computer awareness and applications software to revenue officials for regular updating of records of rights and smooth operation of computer centers. Digitization of maps has also been allowed under the CLR scheme.

Initially, it was decided that basic infrastructure would be created at the district level for undertaking data entry. After completion of data entry (including verification and validation at the district level), data has to be ported to tehsil or taluk computer centers for regular operation. Therefore, in 1997-98 it was decided to extend the scheme to the tehsil or taluk level to facilitate better accessibility to computerized copies of RoRs for landowners.

Phased coverage under the scheme:

- During the VIIth Plan, 24 districts were sanctioned;
- During the VIIIth Plan, an additional 299 districts were sanctioned;
- During the IXth Plan, an additional 259 districts and 2787 tehsils or taluks were sanctioned;
- Tehsils or taluks sanctioned during the first four years of Xth Plan period (2002-03 to 2005-06) are as follows:

The Budget provision during the current financial year viz, 2006-07 under the scheme of CLR is Rs.100.00 crore (Rs. 90.00 crore for States/UTs and Rs.10.00 crore for NE States). As on date, funds to the tune of Rs. 51.14 crore have been released to the states for data entry work and scanning and digitization of land records including cadastral maps.

Since its inception, the scheme has been sanctioned to 582 districts, 3527 taluks/ tehsils and blocks and 1019 subdivisions. In 3324 tehsils, taluks and blocks computer centres have been set up and in 2877 tehsils, taluks and blocks, computerized copies of RoRs are being issued to landowners on demand. Digitization of maps has also been allowed under the scheme.

(Table 6.1: Allocation of Funds)

Year	Sanctioned Locations	Funds released (Rs. in crore)
2002-03	183 taluks	31.18
2003-04	172 taluks, 201 subdivisions and 191 district land records data centers.	35.77
2004-05	178 taluks, 361 subdivisions and 51 district land records data centers	45.62
2005-06	207 taluks, 457 subdivisions and 122 district land records data centers.	99.24
Total	**740 tehsils/taluks, 1019 sub-divisional and 365 district land records data centers**	**211.81**

So far Rs. 496.52 crore have been released to states and union territories of which Rs. 292.52 crore (59%) have been utilized by states/UTs.

Statewise achievements under the CLR scheme

The states of Karnataka, Goa, Tamilnadu and Gujarat have stopped manual distribution of RoRs by totally relying on the computerized system for more than a year now. Many other states are making good progress in shifting to the computerized system. Some States have also placed land records data on the Internet websites for easy access and dissemination of this information.

Goa — This is the first State which has completed land records computerization. The Dharniproject is an integrated system in which mutation has been automated and updated copies of RoRs are being issued to landowners along with locational details. Though legal sanctity has been accorded to computerized copies, issue of manual records has not been stopped because the State is providing computers to the village officers in a phased manner.

Karnataka — The Bhoomi project integrates mutation and update of land records to ensure that RoRs provided to farmers are up to date. The workflow has been automated and secured using security mechanisms. Manual issue of the RoRs has been stopped in 177 taluks and legal sanctity is accorded to computerized RoRs. Under the project, 1.5 crore landowners have taken computerized copies of the RTC from taluk computer centres earning Rs. 22.58 crores as user charges for the State.

Tamilnadu — A computerized land records system called Tamil Nilam is operational. Regular mutation and update is being done through computers. This is an integrated system with interface to other citizen-centric services such as old age pension, lodging complaints relating to mutation, etc. The manual system of issue of RoRs has been abandoned throughout the state.

Gujarat — A computerized land records system called e-Dhara is fully operational with mutation, update and distribution of copies of RoRs is being done through taluk computer centres. The State has notified computerized copies of RoRs as legally valid documents. Digital data of ll districts have been kept at the State level and is hosted on the Internet.

Madhya Pradesh — Computerized copies of the khasra (RoRs) are being distributed in 257 of 273 tehsils on demand. Gram panchayats are empowered to certify undisputed mutations at the village level and other types of mutations are being approved by revenue officials. Efforts are being made to register all mutations on tehsil computers and distribute only computerized copies of RoRs. Land records data have been posted on the website for easy access and display.

Orissa — Data entry work for RoRs has been completed and the scheme is operational in 161 of 171 tehsils where computerized copies of RoRs are being distributed on demand. Land record data have been hosted on website.

West Bengal — Computerized copies of RoRs are being distributed to land owners in all blocks on demand. Manual issue of RoRs have been banned and legal sanctity provided to computerized copies of RoR.

Rajasthan — Copies of computerized *jamabandi* RoRs are being issued in all the 241 tehsils. Land record data is available on the Internet.

Andhra Pradesh — Data entry work has been completed and computerized RoR copies are being distributed in 308 *Mandate,* which are sub-taluk level small revenue units.

Pondicherry — Data entry work has been completed in all taluks and verification is in an advanced stage. The scheme has been made operational in 5 out of 8 taluks and computerized RoR copies are being distributed to landowners on demand.

Sikkim — Data entry has been completed for the entire State, and in 4 sub-divisions distribution of updated copies of RoRs has started.

Chhattisgarh — Computer centres have been set up in all tehsils and computerized copies of RoRs are being distributed to landowners on demand. The land records data has been hosted on the website.

Kerala — 45 per cent data entry has been completed and the balance work is expected to be completed very soon. Computer centres have been set up in all taluks but computerized copies of RoRs are yet to be issued to landowners.

Maharashtra — Computerisation of land records had been completed and all the tehsils are on-line. State government has started distribution of computerized copies of RoRs in all 358 taluks on demand.

Uttar Pradesh — Data entry work alongwith backlog data verification and validation has been completed. Computerized copies of RoRs are being distributed to landowners from all the 305 tehsils. Manual issue of RoRs has been stopped.

Haryana — Data entry work has been completed and verification and validation work is at an advanced stage of completion. The scheme has been operationalized in 67 out of 115 tehsils with issuance of copies of computerized *jamabandis* to landowners on demand. The State has developed an integrated land records and registration system —*Halris,* which enables entry of mutations immediately after registration of land.

Himachal Pradesh — The scheme has been operationalized in 76 out of 108 tehsils with landowners getting computerized copies of RoRs on demand.

Uttarakhand — Computerisation of land records has been completed and the scheme is operational in all 84 tehsils with landowners getting computerized copies of RoRs on demand. Manual issue of RoRs have been stopped. The land records data have been hosted on the website.

NCT of Delhi — Ninety nine per cent data entry work has been completed and computerized copies of RoRs are being issued to landowners.

Assam, Arunachal Pradesh, Mizoram, Manipur, Bihar, Tripura and UTs of Andaman & Nicobar Islands and Chandigarh — Data entry is under progress. Software for mutation and updation through computer centres has been developed by the NIC.

J&K, Punjab, Jharkhand, Nagaland and the UTs of Dadra & Nagar Haveli and Daman & Diu — Data entry has not been completed, and the scheme is yet to gain momentum.

Meghalaya & Lakshadweep — The scheme has not yet started because of non-availability of land records. They have been asked to undertake survey work for creating land records so that the scheme could be implemented.

Centrally Sponsored Scheme of Strengthening of Revenue Administration and Updating of Lard Records (SRA & ULR)

The importance of land records in the rural areas cannot be over-emphasised. The causes of rural conflicts have often been traced to improper maintenance of land records. Updation is vital for systematic maintenance of land records to reflect ownership changes, ensure genuine land transactions and implement rural development programmes for effective enforcement of land reforms. It will minimize land disputes and create social harmony in villages.

Although the importance of a proper land records system has been emphasized from the First Five-Year Plan, land records in most parts of the country are not in good shape largely due to resource constraints. As per existing instructions, records of rights are prepared by carrying out cadastral surveys followed by settlement operations; these are time consuming, call for huge staff and is expensive. Equipment used in these operations is also outdated. Even where there is a system of periodical updating of land records, lack of adequate revenue machinery and proper infrastructure and absence of training are responsible for poorly maintained land records.

To assist the states and UTs in the task of updating of land records and strengthening revenue administration, a centrally sponsored scheme of strengthening of revenue administration and updating of land records (SRA & ULR) was started in 1987-88 on 50:50 sharing basis between the Centre and the states. Union Territories are provided full central assistance. Initially, the scheme was approved for the states of Bihar and Orissa in 1987-88 and 'extended to other states/UTs during 1989-90. The scheme is being implemented by the state governments through their Revenue/Land Reforms Departments.

The main objectives of the scheme are:

(1) Strengthening survey and settlement organizations for early completion and preparation of land records in areas where this work is yet to be completed.

(2) Setting up survey and settlement organizations especially in the north-east, where no land records exist.

(3) Imparting pre-service and in-service training to revenue, survey and settlement staff and strengthening training infrastructure for this purpose.

(4) Providing facilities for modernization of survey and settlement operations, printing survey maps, reports and

documents and storage, copying and updating of land and crop records using, among other things, latest science and technology inputs.

(5) Strengthening revenue machinery at the village and immediate supervisory levels on a selective basis to make the work load of functionaries manageable.

Under the scheme, states and UTs have been given assistance for purchase of modern survey equipment (like Global Positioning Systems, GPS, EDM, total stations, theodolites, work stations), carrying out aerial surveys, office equipment (like photocopiers, laminating machines and binding machines) and basic facilities to improve work efficiency at lower levels of revenue administration, construction of record rooms for proper storage of land records, construction of office-cum-residence for *patwari* and construction, repair and renovation of training institutes and equipment for training.

Tables 6.2 Release of funds during first four years of Xth Plan:

Year	Funds released (Rs. in crore)
2002-03	20.73
2003-04	24.21
2004-05	19.43
2005-06	39.49
Total	**103.86**

A provision of Rs. 49.00 crore (Rs.5.00 crore for NE States and Rs. 44.00 crore for non-NE States) existed under the scheme during the financial year of 2006-07. Funds to the tune of Rs. 8.83 crores were released to the states for purchase of modern survey equipment, continuation of survey works, training of staff, etc.

Since its inception (1987-88), financial assistance to the tune of Rs. 333.72 crore has been provided to state governments and UTs as the Central share, of which Rs. 253.81 crores (76%) have been utilized by the states.

North Eastern Region

Land Reforms Division is implementing the schemes of computerisation of land records (CLR) and strengthening of revenue administration and updating of Land Records (SRA&ULR) in the region.

National Land Resources Management Programme (NLRMP)

Significant progress has been made by the states and UTs under the existing two centrally sponsored schemes of computerisation of land records (CLR) and strengthening of revenue administration and updating of land records (SRA & ULR) in the field of computerization and digitization of land records, strengthening of survey and settlement organizations by purchase of equipments of various kinds including modern survey equipment such as global positional systems (GPS), electronic total stations (ETS), maintenance and storage of land records by construction of record rooms, improvement in training infrastructure for revenue and survey staff by construction/ renovation of new/existing training institutes etc. However, the emphasis of CLR and SRA & ULR so far, has *inter alia* been more on computerization and digitization of land records, strengthening of state revenue, survey and settlement organisations, maintenance and storage of land records and less on having a system that maintains accurate and up to date records of rights and securely generates such records on demand. Also lacking, are the integration of textual and spatial data on RoRs, linkage of registration with mutation and updating of RoRs, back-end reconciliation of village records, and a comprehensive and standard database of land records across the country that is necessary for understanding land and immovable property markets and for efficient administration and policymaking in a modern economy.

Further, some progress has been made in a number of states in computerization of the property registration. However, the prime focus of these initiatives has been on automation of the deed registration procedures, and there is hardly any link with the land records management system.

Keeping in mind the overarching goal of comprehensive and all-round development, the key deliverables that need to be provided to our citizens would include computerized RoRs with maps to scale, other land data based certificates e.g. domicile certificate, caste certificate, income certificate, and also the necessary documents/information for securing agricultural and non-agricultural credit based on land assets and so on.

With this backdrop, a National Land Resources Management Programme (NLRMP) has been conceptualized as a major e-governance and system reforms initiative that is concerned not merely with the computerization, updation and maintenance of land records or the validation of titles, but as a programme that will add value and provide a comprehensive data base for planning and decision making for development planning as well as regulatory activities where there is need for location-specific information. The disconnects and redundancies in the system would be reduced and a better reform model would be re-engineered, so that the spatial and non-spatial land-related data for the entire country could be available as a national enterprise knowledge base for both public and private stakeholders.

The NLRMP will, *inter alia,* focus on citizen services like computerized records of rights (RoRs) with maps; certificates (domicile, caste, income, etc.); web-based "anytime-anywhere" access to land data; services through facilitation centres in tehsils and other places; speedy and efficient property registration; automatic initiation of mutation notices; land passbooks — smart cards with all land information including charges and encumbrances; facilitated access to land-based credit/cooperative banks, etc. It envisages creation of core GIS with cadastral layer for the entire country, 100 per cent digitization of cadastral maps, integration of textual and spatial data, updating of land records using modern technology (aerial photogrammetry, DGPS, ETS), National and State Land Data Banks with specific plot IDs and details, use of uniform land data codes with Indian language script computing, integration with National spatial database (NSDB) and National natural resources management system (NNRMS), full training and capacity building of the functionaries and national and state missions for effective implementation.

This comprehensive programme to manage land data and information will support the entire spectrum of land resource management, and all developmental, regulatory and disaster management activities needing location-specific information will be benefited.

7
Functioning of Naxalite Outfits

Maoist Communist Centre was formed in 1969 after Amulya Sen and Kanai Chatterjee parted with Charu Mazumdar who believed in annihilating the class enemies. Sen and Chatterjee emphasized on public movement. It is a different story that later on MCC itself took recourse to direct action to finish the so-called class enemies. Initially, they indulged in settlement of local dispute by force, threatening big landlords, illegal realization from forest contractors, killing of informers and indulging in arson and blast.

MCC has three frontal organizations: (a) Party organization, (b) Force/army organization and (c) People organization.

The organization has, areawise, special area committees for Bihar-Bengal, Assam-Tripura, Bihar-Uttar Pradesh, Bengal-Orissa and Andhra Pradesh-Orissa. Party at various levels has corresponding militia organization. It has people's organizations in the names of Revolutionary Farmers Committee, Revolutionary Cultural Organization, Women Liberation Association, Communist Young League, Farmers' Movement Front, Labourers Liberation Organization, Revolutionary Students' League, Intellectuals Organization etc. from village level to Central Committee level. There are members and office bearers, areawise, for each committee or organization.

Similarly Peoples War Group (PWG) has organizational set up from central committee, special zonal committee (at the state level), regional committee, divisional committee, area committee and down to the village committee. This was established in 1980 and has spread to Telengana region of Andhra Pradesh, Orissa, Chhattisgarh, Jharkhand and few parts of Karnataka. It has militant organization at the platoon level (approx. 30 heads), SGS (about 15 heads) and LGS (about eight-nine heads). They have the latest weaponry and are expert in guerrilla warfare. They have women members who successfully incite public for violence. Two other Naxalite organizations are CPI (ML) (Vinod Mishra) and CPI(ML) Party Unity (PU). CPI(ML) (VM) is well equipped with men and arms, yet it believes in taking part in election process.

MCC aims at publicising their ideology so that people in large number may get associated with the party. They want to identify movable and immovable properties of capitalists and to forcibly usurp on them. On police intervention, the weapons of police force are snatched after attacking them. After taking possession of land of big landowners, they allow their members to cultivate those lands and even realize money from the landowners as levy.

Their strategy is to include local people in their organization and continue warfare with their support to expose ruling class by describing their luxurious ways of life and to take local populace into confidence before starting guerilla warfare. Once they declare any area as guerilla zone, they administer at the village level through their supporters, by giving armed protection through various armed guerilla formations.

PWG specially utilize landmines to cause large number of casualties of the police force which also facilitates them to loot police arms. This is a greater demoralising strategy than the ambush or attack by encircling the police force. Sometimes they come as labourers and sometimes in other disguises. One section engages the sentry of the police outpost whereas others take position to launch a full-fledged assault. Very often they come in disguise at the police station to give sensitive information of Naxalite attack, rape, murders or dacoity and then take advantage of the empty police outpost and run away with arms and ammunitions. When they plan to attack any prison or police station or police lines in a subdivisional or district headquarter, they forcibly take villagers along with them to act as human shield for them. They occupy government vacant land, forest land and benami lands. They do not allow the sale of these lands. They hold people's courts in villages and settle local disputes amicably. They enroll disgruntled unemployed youths by convincing them about the failures of governments, kidnap officials to pressurize local administration, burn down roadways, buses, railway stations or telephone centres, scare away police informers, zamindars and contractors by causing explosions nearby, attack police station, call bandh or road blockade to show their strength with a purpose to participate in political process ultimately.

To run their large organizational structure, they extort money from the landowners, moneyed men and the contractors. They execute their action in the following four phases;

1. Identify the area.
2. Develop contacts with the local people of that area to make them their supporters.
3. Commit serious offences by forming of the group
4. Form the liberated zone.

In the liberated zone, they run parallel administration and extort money from the contractors and government officials. If the defined person does not pay, he is killed. They, however, continue to strengthen their armoury by books and works.

Recruitment

They lure young villagers to come to their fold by offering them monthly remuneration or by giving them financial assistance apart from brainwashing them into their ideology. Sometimes, the people from the oppressed class join these organizations to take revenge against the powerful class who have been harassing and exploiting them so far. Once they join their organization, they have to strictly follow their diction and discipline or drill. If someone violates, they will kill him first than their class enemy. They strictly follow discipline to respect women and to follow the local customs, cultural rituals and local behaviour.

They have their selected training centres which are generally located in the dense forest. The trainers generally come from Andhra Pradesh. Training is from one to two months and is given to a centre who has completed minimum tenure successfully which may range from six months to one year.

Thus they build up an organization which will be militarily strong and politically sound. For that they make their cadres physically tough and mentally alert. Thus, a naxalite organization seeks to create full organization which can run parallel to the government organization. Apart from regular army training, the cadres are also given classes for their educational improvement.

Strategy

They do not surrender because Comrade Charu Mazumder said that the surrender tantamounts to suicide. Similarly, Comrade Mao said that the attack is the best defence. They adopt three tactics of assault. First, it is the raid which is resorted to as "hit and run" tactics so that they may create panic in the police force and can run away with their arms and ammunitions and to kill a selected police officer, cruel landowner, middleman or political leader. Second, attack is organized when some important comrades are to be released from the police custody or from jails. Third is ambush. After ambush, the members of assault group hide themselves within 50/60 mtrs. distance so that they can finish enemies by way of continuous firing or grenade attack.

As Naxalites are well aware of the terrain they take position at a place so that they can see the police force clearly whereas the police or para-military force cannot see them clearly as the latter is equipped with more sophisticated arms like LMG, machine gun, grenade etc.

The Naxal groups are experts in laying the mines as the area is in their control. The village roads are not pucca. It is where the most powerful police or para-military force is scared of these extremists groups. Even use of helicopters could not help them to locate the extremist's groups because they go under the forest or cave corner. They disguise themselves as army or paramilitary personnel to blend in with their surrondings. Besides they have their network of local informers who facilitate their activities. Which is why it took decades for Tamilnadu and Karnataka police to kill the brigand Veerappan.

Sources of their income:

1. Ransom after kidnapping of government officials or local rich people.
2. Usurpation of lands of rich landowners.
3. Collecting subscription for the local people by luring them to their fold.
4. Realizing the proceeds by giving forest or government lands on lease.
5. Taking levy from rich persons and traders.
6. Selling forest or mineral produce lying in government stockyard.
7. Realing the levy from government officials and officers.

But their expenditures are well regulated. They keep the accounts of each rupee. If one indulges in dishonesty, he is simply killed. Thus, corruption has not yet crept into Naxal organizations though they are operating on the same Indian soil. Their lifestyle is also simple. Leaders and cadres lead same type of simple living.

As per police reports, vices of drinking, gambling, sex-exploitation, and comforts form a part of their lifestyle. They have PT in the morning and drill in the evening. Thus they have four hours of physical training. They have classes for three hours before lunch and two hours during night. With such a regular life, no cadre likes to come out of the Naxal outfit.

There are magazines like *Lai Pataka*, *Lal Chingari*, *Krantikari Geetmala*, *Bigul Masik Samachar*, *Jan Jwar*, *Struggling Forum for Peoples Resistance* that are published regularly. These carry their activities throughout Indian and even foreign countries like Nepal, Philippine, Peru etc. They put more focus on police atrocities so that cadres become keen to gain revenge from the police force.

They ultimately want to bring bloody revolution on the pattern of revolution brought about by Mao Zedong. They start by advocating the cases of poor cultivators or landless persons in the villages, but ultimately the main aim gets diluted and one sees armed struggle all-around for land and basic facilities in villages are met. The violence can, to a large extent, come down as the Naxalites then, will not be able to muster strong support from the common people. Today, they have all points to exploit them. Thus, this is high time to understand their strategy and to make best efforts to meet their genuine demands. If they do not come to terms, they cannot defeat the modern sophisticated well armed state specially in a large country like India.

It is also alleged that along with ideology of Mao and Marx, the Naxalites receive foreign assistance. But their main aim was and is agrarian struggle to distribute land to the poor. For that they mobilize poor peasants. They killed many bitterly hated landlords only after trials were held in people's courts. They want to establish or seize power in their base areas. Thus, they are also very clear that unlike success of Naxalism in small country like Nepal, they cannot seize political power in small states let alone whole country. For the time being their violent campaign in small states like Chhatisgarh and Jharkhand is successful but when the armed forces lay siege on them, they will be helpless. Central Government and state governments are raising lakh of armed soldiers to fight a combined Naxal force of not more than 12,000 personnel. In fact, the Naxalite movement is fast spreading though it may not be as sophisticated and well equipped as the police forces are. It is because of their exalted aim to ensure right of cultivation to the rural poor. Violence etc is to achieve that main aim. However, on many occasions it gets derailed and misdirected as it is not a scientifically led movement or force.

The armed struggles that began in Naxalbari in North Bengal were aimed at restoring the rights of the agricultural labour in tea gardens by enabling them to become owners of the land that, till then, they had been cultivating for the powerful and established landlords of the area. With the objective of making the exploited cultivators the owners of the land on which they work, this movement quickly spread from the coastal plains of Srikakulam in Andhra Pradesh to Sonbhadra in Uttar Pradesh and from the Santhal Parganas in Jharkhand to Dantewala in Chhattisgarh. According to a report of the Social Council for Social Development, this armed struggle has spread to 170 of the total 607 districts in the country. This means that the law and order situation in one fourth of the country has reached a low level. Crores of rupees are spent to tackle the problem of Naxalism in a firefighting manner but no permanent solution like land reforms is being initiated by the affected governments. Even the proposals for land reforms are put forward here and there, but there seems to be no listeners leave alone the takers. They only listen from the nozzle of the gun or from the blast of gun powder. For example, since the creation of the State of Chhattisgarh in 2000, the State government has made no voluntary effort for restoring or distributing land to its landless tribals. In 2003, after a prolonged movement by a people's organization in Kanwardhah district of Chhattisgarh, the government announced distribution of land to 6,100 families of the Baiga Tribe but since then only 40 per cent of the distribution has been completed. On the other hand in the last six years an estimated 42,000 acres of land has been acquired for industrial purpose in the tribal dominated districts of Sarguja, Kanwardhah and Raigadh.

Land acquisition is a new weapon in the hands of Naxal organizations. It is a fact that police forces are quick to nab their theoreticians, thinkers, guides, moral supporters from the urban hideouts but the police can hardly make impact on Naxalite outfits in far-flung forests living with people's support. The Indian people are basically peace loving, more so the farmers. Therefore, the Naxalite movement will lose base where it has been active without any tangible benefits to the local people. The people even in Jammu and Kashmir are fed up with consistent incidents of violence. Sometimes, they also lose their kith and kins in crossfiring.

They have to part with their paltry food items to the volunteers or cadrcs of Naxalites. Lastly, sometimes their women are also exploited either by Naxals or by the police force. This expedites their fast turning towards peaceful democratic society. They become mentally prepared to tolerate certain amount of corruption, nepotism and inefficiency in the system than constant gunfire or bloodshed.

As a result, the Naxalite movement is fast moving to new areas. Its avowed object is not questionable. But like government policy, it does not get implemented in practice.

Naxalites are adopting new strategies, and weapons to spread their movement. Government should also change its strategy from negative to positive so that the Naxalite problem is solved once for all. They should not view Naxalites as their enemies or red terrorists but the ones who have challenged them in their sleep to rise and deliver justice to the rural poor specially the Dalits and the Adivasis.

The villagers are the worst hit in crossfires. A villager has rightly remarked, "Between the government and the Naxalites, without doubt, government is a better alternative but till the time, a democratic government reached my village and my doorstep, the Naxalites are definitely preferable".

However the violence which is order of the day, should be avoided at all costs.

8
Strategy to Tackle Naxalism

The present strategy to tackle extremist outfits is a simple fire fighting mechanism based on police report and by the police. There is hardly any input from the radical thinker, civil servants and statesman politicians.

The police organizations furnish so much intelligence information that it leaves no gap or scope to the policy-planners or top executives to think otherwise. Directorate of Intelligence Bureau is one of the best organized networks in the country. It has store of readymade information, which emerges from the ground level informer who is not much educated. With the police orientation of his mind for number of years, he cannot think otherwise except to meet violence by violence. Secondly, during his term with the police organization, he has not come across land reform measures being implemented in the field. The very mentality of police is negative which genuinely feels that there is nothing good in the society. Whatever small good they can do, is the only alternative. Through such an apparatus, the information filters and reaches in a very well-couched language on the table of the minister through the secretary of the department. In spite of his best intentions, secretary, will not like to give his own inputs as the police bosses will prove him wrong if any of his suggestion goes faulty. The top brass of the police have easy access to the top political executive and they certainly bypass the civil service secretary. Therefore, the path of least resistance for the secretary is to pass the papers as they are received from the intelligence wing of the police force. As a result, strategy is finalized to meet violence by the state violence, tooth for tooth and an eye for an eye. Ultimately, the Naxalite violence has to be encountered by the police or para-military force. Therefore, the easy strategy is to approve a plan of action, which the executor or implementation agency is the best equipped to adopt and which they demand. Some of the conscientious police officers raise dissenting voice, but their voice is not heard and sometimes it is suppressed as theoretical, academic or outdated. The ministry of home affairs is managed mostly by the civil service officers, yet the strategy finalized by them does not show any civil input whatsoever.

The Naxalite uprising is the most dangerous uprising which has claimed more lives than any other incidents or operation or even wars after independence. The figures from 2003 to 31.10.06 are as follows:

1.	Personnel of Police force or para-military force killed	492
2.	Civilians killed	1876
3.	Naxalites killed/untraceable	736
4.	Incidents	6610
5.	No. of Naxalite arrested	5667
6.	No. of Naxalites surrendered	4890

One has to pause for a while and think why innocent villagers are lured into the fold of extremists. All are not taken by force or are blackmailed. It is a happy sign that this realization of late, is dawning upon the bureaucrats sitting in North Block, New Delhi. The ministry of home affairs is asking various other departments to push up their developmental plans in the Naxalite affected far-flung regions hitherto neglected for whatever reasons and also to undertake people specific schemes specially for tribals and scheduled castes of those regions who form the majority of the Naxalite groups or outfits. But one fails to understand why the ministry of home affairs does not release funds from their own coffers. The problem is theirs. Other departments are busy with their routine schemes and works. Rather than raising battalions of para-military forces and purchasing sophisticated arms for them, they should earmark a percentage of fund for developmental activities in Naxal affected regions. The response from other departments of Central Government, including state governments is also lukewarm because they have not been clearly explained or told how serious the problem is. They must be made to realize that they would not be able to carry out any of their developmental plans if the district administration at the grass root level gets constantly engaged tackling the Naxalite problem. After all, machinery to channelise all schemes of all departments is one. That is district administration in India. Naxals have still not lost faith in civil administration of the district though they have lost faith in election process and also in panchayat bodies because panchayat bodies play partisan roles in the rural India. If panchayats execute schemes impartially and honestly, the Naxalite problem can be tackled by them. The rest of the job can be accomplished by the revenue department or land and land reforms department under influence of the vested interest or to hide their inefficiency or due to lack of political or administrative will, they keep on repeating that land reforms have been completed and nothing is left to be done. Even if they take one agenda namely to identify the patta-holders or assignees of vested lands to ensure that real possession of government surplus land given to them, it will take at least five years to accomplish this primary or basic agenda or component of land reform. Land reform is a continuous process and is never ending. It will end only when all the poor men on land have-nots are brought at par with the haves and an egalitarian rural society comes up on surface asserting its identity and power as any other segment of the society.

Let us examine what strategy has been adopted by the Government of India and circulated to the state governments for guidance to bring down the rigour of Naxal violence in the country mainly as security centric measures.

As per the report appearing in *Telegraph* [Kolkata dt. 23.05.08],[1] the Maoists have widened their network three fold in the past two years, spreading to 183 districts from 55 in 2005 across 16 states. In fact, fully Naxal affected districts are 76 only in India as on date as per a more specific survey and information submitted to Parliament.

The home ministry lists Kerala, Tamilnadu, Punjab, Haryana, Uttarakhand, Uttar Pradesh and Delhi as the states where the Maoists have established new bases by setting up regional and district-level centres. The strength of the armed Maoists Cadre, too has risen from 8000 in 2005 and 11,000 in 2006 to 15,000 in 2007.

Policy to deal with the Naxalite menace

The present policy of the Government of India comprises the following components –

1. The Government will deal sternly with the naxalites indulging in violence.
2. Keeping in view that Naxalism is not merely a law and order problem, the policy of the Government is to handle this menace simultaneously on political, security, development and public perception management fronts in a holistic manner.
3. Naxalism being an interstate problem, the states will adopt a collective approach and pursue a coordinated response to counter it.
4. The states will need to further improve police response and pursue effective and sustained police action against Naxalites and their infrastructure individually and jointly.
5. There will be no peace dialogue by the affected states with the Naxal groups unless the latter agree to give up violence through arms.
6. Political parties must strengthen their cadre base in Naxal affected areas so that the potential youth there can be weaned away from the path of Naxal ideology.
7. The states from where Naxal activity/influence, and not Naxal violence, is reported should have a different approach with special focus on accelerated socio-economic development of the backward areas and regular interaction with NGOs, intelligentsia, civil liberties groups, etc., to minimize over ground support for the Naxalite ideology and activity.
8. Efforts will continue to be made to promote voluntary local resistance groups against Naxalites but in a manner that the villagers are provided adequate security cover and the area is effectively dominated by the security forces.

9. Mass media should be extensively used to highlight the futility of Naxal ideology and violence and loss of life and property caused by it and development schemes of the government in the affected areas so as to restore people's faith and confidence in the government machinery.
10. The states should announce a suitable transfer policy for the Naxal affected districts. Willing, committed and competent officers with greater delegation of authority need to be posted with a stable tenure in the Naxal affected districts. Delegation of more power will enable them to deliver better and step up government presence and above all improve governance in these areas.
11. The Government of Andhra Pradesh has an effective surrender and rehabilitation policy for Naxalites and has produced good results over the years. The other states should adopt a similar policy.
12. The state governments will need to accord a higher priority in their annual plans to ensure faster socio-economic development of the Naxal affected areas. The focus areas should be to distribute land to the landless poor as part of the speedy implementation of land reforms, ensure development of physical infrastructure like roads, communication, power etc. and provide employment opportunities to the youth in these areas.
13. Another related issue is that development activities are not undertaken in some of the Naxalite affected areas due to extortion, threat or fear from their cadres. In these areas, even contractors are not coming forward to take up developmental work. Adequate security and other measures are required to facilitate un-interrupted developmental activities in the Naxal affected areas.
14. The Central Government will continue to supplement the efforts and resources of the affected states on both security and development fronts for coordination between the states to successfully tackle the problem.

Countermeasures

While the overall counteraction by the affected states in terms of Naxalites killed, arrested, surrendered and arms recovered from them achieved better results in 2005 and 2006 so far, there is an urgent need to further improve and strengthen police response particularly by the states of Chhattisgarh, Jharkhand, Bihar, Orissa and Maharashtra by improving actionable intelligence collection and sharing mechanism and strengthening their police forces on the pattern of SIB and Greyhounds in Andhra Pradesh. Unfortunately, 38 Greyhound commandos were killed in Naxalite attack on 30.06.2008 while they were crossing a water body in Malkangiri district of Orissa.

Police Response

In order to supplement the efforts of the states in providing an effective response to the Naxal violence, Central Para Military Forces have been deployed on a long-term basis as requested by the affected states. The Central Government has also exempted the states from the payment of cost of deployment of these forces for a period of three years from 01.07.04 involving an amount of over Rs. 1200 crores.

The Naxal affected states have been sanctioned India Reserve (IR) battalions mainly to strengthen security apparatus at their level and also to enable them to provide gainful employment to the youth, particularly in the Naxal areas. Recently, ten additional IR battalions have also been approved for the Naxal affected states. The Central Government will now provide Rs. 20.75 crores per IR battalion as against the earlier amount of Rs. 13 crores per battalion. The states have been asked to expedite raising of these battalions.

Recruitment in Central Para Military Forces

In order to wean away the potential youths from the path to militancy or Naxalism, recruitment guidelines have been revised to permit 40 per cent recruitment in Central Para Military Forces from the border areas and areas affected by militancy or Naxalism.

Salva Judum in Bastar Region, Chhattisgarh

Salva Judum — an anti-Naxal movement began in June 2005 in Bastar region of Chhattisgarh as a spontaneous expression of pent up anti-Naxalite sentiments among the local people. The movement was triggered by a meeting of eight villages at Teomar village under PS Kutru of police district Bijapur, where the villagers expressed their unhappiness with the modus operandi of Naxalites causing harassment and starvation of common villagers due to the deprival of employment opportunities. Salva Judum activists mobilized villagers/tribals against Naxals through a series of rallies, meetings and padyatras in Naxal strongholds of the two blocks [Bijapur and Bhairamgarh] of Bijapur police district in South Bastar. This voluntary and peaceful movement by local people has now spread into Bijapur, Bhairamgarh, Usoor, Sukma and Konta blocks in Dantewada district. Salva Judum activists held more than 150 anti-Naxalite rallies.

The spread of Salva Judum beyond the Bhairamgarh and Bijapur blocks of Dantewada district, into the West (Usoor block) and the south (Konta and Sukma blocks) of Dantewada district (bordering Andhra Pradesh) seems to have caused a major setback to the CPI (Maoist), who had hitherto been enjoying a complete dominance in the area. Naxalites have thus resorted to killing, of civilians/tribals to threaten Salva Judum activists with an aim to derail the Salva Judum campaign.

Keeping in view the importance of Salva Judum movement as a major bulwark in sustained campaign against Naxals and in view of the Naxalite attacks on innocent Salva Judum activists, the state government has been advised to enhance the deployment of security forces to provide effective area domination, ensure safety of Salva Judum activists and strengthen security of relief camps.

Backward Districts Initiative [BDI]

Since the Naxalite menace has to be addressed on the developmental front also, the Central Government has provided financial assistance of Rs. 2,475 crores for 55 Naxal affected districts in nine states of Andhra Pradesh, Bihar, Chhattisgarh, Orissa, Jharkhand, Maharashtra, Madhya Pradesh, Uttar Pradesh and West Bengal under the backward districts initiative (BDI) component of the Rashtriya Sam Vikas Yojana (RSVY). Under the scheme, an amount of Rs. 15 crores per year has been given to each of the districts for three years to fill in critical gaps in physical and social development in the Naxal affected areas. Apart from these districts, other Naxal affected areas/districts have also been included under the Backward Regions Grant Fund (BRGF) Scheme which covers 250 backward districts in the country and has an outlay of nearly Rs. 4,000 crores from the fiscal year (2006-07) onwards.

Tribal and Forest Related Issues

In order to address the areas of disaffection among the tribals, the Government had introduced the Scheduled Tribes [Recognition of Forest Rights] Bill 2005, in Parliament on 13.12.05 which has now become an Act. Further, to facilitate social and physical infrastructure in the forest areas, Ministry of Environment and Forests has, as requested by the MHA, issued general approval to allow such infrastructure by utilizing up to 1 hectare of forest land for non-forest purposes. That ministry has also permitted upgrade of kutcha roads constructed prior to 01.09.80 into pucca roads.

Land Reforms and Creation of Employment Opportunities

Naxal groups have been raising mainly land and livelihood related issues. If land reforms are taken up on priority and the landless and the poor in the Naxal areas are allotted surplus land, this would go a long way in tackling the developmental aspects of the Naxal problem. The states have been requested to focus greater attention on this area and also accelerate people centric developmental activities and create employment opportunities in the Naxal affected areas with special focus on creation of infrastructure in terms of roads, communication, power along with social infrastructure such as schools, hospitals, etc.

Monitoring Mechanisms

The Central Government accords a very high priority to review and monitor the Naxal situation and the measures being taken by the states on both security and development fronts to control it. Several monitoring mechanisms have been set up at the Centre for this purpose. These include a periodical review by the Cabinet Committee on Security (CCS) of the Naxal situation, a Standing Committee of the chief ministers of the Naxal affected states chaired by the Union home minister. Quarterly Coordination Centre meetings chaired by the Union home secretary with the chief secretaries and the directors general of police of the affected states and the monthly task force meetings of Nodal officers of Naxal affected states and central agencies taken by special secretary (IS), MHA. The states have also been asked to hold a monthly review by the DGP and a bimonthly review by the chief secretary on the Naxal situation and the measures and strategies taken to contain the Naxal problem on both security and development fronts.

Meeting of the Standing Committee of Chief Ministers of Naxal affected States

The second meeting of the Standing Committee of the chief ministers of Naxal affected states was held in New Delhi on 13.04.06 under the chairmanship of the Prime Minister. While, on the security front, the meeting, *inter alia,* underlined the need for building up security and intelligence capabilities at state and district levels for effective and sustained anti-Naxal operations and for preparation/revision and implementation of long-term action plans to address the security and development aspects of the Naxalite problem, better coordination between RPF, GRP, local police and other agencies to ensure safety of railway passengers, trains and other railway infrastructure, the agenda items on the development front, comprised need for better delivery and monitoring mechanisms in Naxal areas, effective implementation of land reforms, formulation of rehabilitation and resettlement (RR) policy for displaced tribals, speedy implementation of the Panchayats (Extension to Scheduled Areas) Act [PESA] 1996 etc.

Inter-ministerial Group (IMG)

An Inter-ministerial Group (IMG) has been set up under the chairmanship of Additional Secretary (ANC) to closely review and address the socio-economic aspects of the Naxal problem. The IMG comprises joint secretary level officers of the main development ministers/departments of the Government of India. The IMG team will also undertake field visits to help improve overall ground level implementation of developmental schemes particularly in the Naxal affected areas.

Chief Ministers meeting on Internal Security

The Prime Minister held a meeting of the chief ministers on internal security on September 5, 2006 and after detailed deliberations the following decisions were taken to combat the Naxal problem :

1. There was unanimity amongst the participants that terrorism and Naxalism need to be dealt with firmly. Closer cooperation among states and between the Centre and states is a must to deal with the wide array of complex internal security problems and threats.
2. To effectively deal with terrorists and Naxalites, the states agreed to take time-bound steps to improve the quality of the state special branches with special focus on tactical and local intelligence generation. The importance of intelligence collection at the police station level was also emphasized.
3. An empowered group of ministers, to be headed by the home minister and comprising select Union ministers and chief ministers will be set up to closely monitor the spread of Naxalism and evolve effective strategies to deal with the problem.

Empowered Group of Ministers (EGoM)

At the ministerial level, an empowered group of ministers (EGoM) with chief ministers of Naxal affected states headed by the Union home minister has been constituted pursuant to the decision taken in the chief ministers' meeting on internal security taken by the Prime Minister on 05.09.2006, to closely monitor the spread of Naxalism and evolve effective strategies to deal with the problem.

Anti-Naxalite Cell/Division

Recently, an anti-Naxal cell headed by additional secretary has been set up in the MHA with a view to ensure periodic review and close monitoring of the action plans drawn up by the states to deal with the Naxal problem. The additional secretary will be assisted by senior civil and police officers and these officers will frequently visit the states and make coordinated efforts to advise and guide the state government officials to effectively deal with the Naxal problem.

In nutshell

The Central Government views the Naxalite menace as an area of serious concern. The Government remains firmly committed and determined to address the problem. Essentially, the state governments would need to pursue effective measures to further improve ground level policing and development response, besides countering the negative propaganda unleashed by Naxalites to contain and control this menace. The Central Government will continue to coordinate and supplement the efforts and resources of the state governments on both security and development fronts to meet the challenge posed by Naxalism.

A NEW APPROACH

The report[2] 'Development challenges in extremist affected areas', authorized by an expert group set up by the Planning Commission, looks at the Naxalite/Maoist movement in a way that is different from the prevalent official attitude and draws attention to many of the positive effects of the movement. The report rejects the official "Security Centric" approach in dealing with the movement and instead suggests an ameliorative approach with emphasis on a negotiated solution.

The expert group headed by D Bandyopadhyay of 'Operation Barga' fame in West Bengal, lays stress on the "structural violence which is implicit in the social and economic system and which in the opinion of its authors prompts the radical groups to justify their own violent acts.

From the investigation carried out by the Planning Commission group of experts in the Naxalite areas, it appears that the Maoists are actually carrying out the reforms that the executive ought to have implemented, and are replacing the judiciary and the police by ensuring law and order for the poor and the oppressed. Commenting on the "Peoples Courts" set up by the Naxalites in these areas of control, the report observes that disputes are resolved in a rough and ready manner, and generally in the interest of the weaker party.

Their findings also reveal how despite change of government, successive rulers who get elected use and misuse laws to suppress the poor and the disadvantaged. There is a design behind this continuity. The elected representatives, irrespective of party affiliations, are not interested in implementing pro-poor legal measures. For instance, the Government of Andhra Pradesh sat with the then People's War Group [now merged into Communist Party of India, Maoist] in October, 2004, and agreed to a ceasefire till Dec. 16 that year, and promised to consider in the meantime the Naxalites' main demand for distribution of land among the landless. But when the then Congress government failed to keep that promise, the Naxalites stepped in to forcibly distribute the land. The government retaliated immediately by sending its police which gunned down Naxalite cadres in the forests of Warangal, West Godavari and other districts in January 2005, writes Sumanta Banerjee[3] in EPW of May 24-30, 2008.

The demand for redistribution of land is the basic demand, which the landless people have right to raise as the land originally belonged to the community [Henry Maine] and it was only through operation of unjust system, some people happen to own more lands than others. Secondly, this is the undisputed and well-declared policy of Central and state governments through all the successive ten Five-Year Plans. Thirdly, this is the simplest administrative manoeuvre because surplus lands have already come into the custody of the state governments by operation of ceiling laws, which have constitutional protection under Schedule IX of the Constitution of India and are immune from challenge in judicial courts. Fourthly, the people below poverty line [BPL] have already been identified in every village in India. Only people without land or less than 1 acre of land are to be listed out and the list approval by the PRIs or the revenue authorities. Rest of the work will be done by the revenue officials who have an arch expertise in the field working since the days of Akbar, the great Mughal.

If popular governments avoid this simple administrative work just because the vested interests of a handful of people will be hurt, they have no legitimate right to be in power. They have to care for dumb majority of the country who have now picked up arms against their double standard and the rest are in the process of taking up arms against the so-called democratic governments. Land is the dearest asset to the villagers because they do not part with land unlike assets from other developmental schemes, which temporarily enrich them and give them pleasure. But sometimes, they also leave them in debt trap. Therefore, even in this era of economic liberalization, the land is the most important ambition of the villagers. Popular governments should pool their resources to purchase the land and distribute the same among the landless or poor villagers. They should do this on the model of "Homestead and Kitchen Garden Scheme" in West Bengal. If the persons at the helm of affairs take the required measures, the existing availability of land in government land bank will suffice for next ten years. But this has to be done in the mission mode approach unlike the routine revenue administration which is almost busy only in mutations and conversions of land and making land titles available for the needs of industries and commerce. The revenue machinery has to arise, recognize their age-old friends in villages and care for them as they are at present at the worst crossroad of history.

Alongwith distribution of land, measures for improvement of lands given under the Bhoodan or wasteland should be undertaken on the pattern of Prime Minister Rozgar Yojna or P.M. Sarak Yojna. This will check the migration of the village poor to the urban areas and to the richer areas or states. After distribution of land, next important step to be taken up is recording sharecroppers without conferring on them the right of ownership. This is also a purely procedural scheme without involvement of any resources. Few more staff and officers will have to be placed with the revenue machinery or with the survey and settlement wing. This can be easily done by diverting surplus staff and officers from many government departments, which have become obsolete or inactive after economic liberalization like food department, urban development or housing boards or authorities, some regulatory wings of labour department etc.

A high-powered National Land Reforms Council [NLRC][4] has been set up under the Prime Minister to make recommendations for completion of unfinished agenda on Land Reforms in the country. Another committee has been set up under the minister of rural development, Government of India. The committee has divided the work among fresh working groups, which will submit their reports and recommendations after field visits and even flying visits. Then these recommendations will be debated before the full committee. The report of the committee will then be finally considered by the high-powered council headed by the Prime Minister. It is expected that some concrete recommendations will emerge from this mega exercise and then these recommendations will be forwarded for implementation to the state governments who will again deliberate in their cabinet. There should be no difficulties in adoption and implementation of these reports because many chief ministers are members of the Council under the Prime Minister.

This is a great step forward that the Central Government for the first time is setting up a mission type organization under the department of land resources, ministry of rural development, which will closely follow up and monitor implementation of recommendations of the council under the Prime Minister. Otherwise these recommendations will gather dust in the department like the other past reports and recommendations. The point to be kept in mind that the officers to be selected for this mission mode organization should be experts in the field of land reforms and are devoted to the cause of the land reform. The dry and dragging field of land reform will not generate interest among careerists and high profile officers and staff except for ulterior motive.

In conclusion, we can say that at this juncture, the political will is required which will take long term interests of the nation into consideration instead of local, narrow or short-term gain or interests.

References

[1] *The Telegraph,* Calcutta 23rd May 2007 under title 'Red run – 7 to 16 States in two years, published by AB Group of Newspapers, Kolkata.

[2] *The Financial Express,* New Delhi, October 29 2007 under the heading "Manmohan to head Land Reforms Council".

[3] Banerjee, Sumanta *'On the Naxalite Movement: A Report with difference',* EPW, vol XLIII No. 21, May 24-30, 2008, Mumbai-400 013.

[4] *Annual Report 2007–08* Government of India, Ministry of Department of Internal Security, North Block Secretariat, New Delhi-110001.

9

Land Reforms in West Bengal

It has been proved beyond doubt that one of the repercussions of non-implementation of land reforms was the growth of 'Naxalite' movement. The surfacing of the Naxalite movement in 1966 in West Bengal and its positive ending by the Left Front Government in West Bengal by implementing land reform measures has proved this case in point very clearly.

The movement did not bring any immediate results in West Bengal and was short-lived but had far reaching implications and became a force behind numerous peasant struggles in different areas of West Bengal, Bihar, Jharkhand (by tribals), Chhatisgarh (by tribals), Andhra Pradesh and Punjab. However, the Left Front Government led by CPI(M) in its three successive terms starting from 1977 salvaged the situation by recording about fifteen lacs share-croppers known as bargadar under "Barga operation" programme. This was consolidated by proper distribution of surplus lands to the landless and by providing bank credits. "For example, up to 1978, in 6 years total 74,000 people got crop-finance whereas in the year 1976 alone 59,000 got crop-finance. Thus, the Communist Government in West Bengal has consolidated its position, which is envied by even Central Government and other state governments".[1]

The West Bengal Scenario

In West Bengal, the implementation of land reform under the Left rule from 1977 has stabilized the rural society, e.g. the average size of land holding was .99 hectares in 1976–77, which has come down to .82 hectares in 2000-01. The land held by marginal farmers has increased. In 1976-77, it was 14.18 lakh hectares whereas in 2000-01 it has grown up to 27.59 lakh hectares. Similarly, the land held by small farmers has also grown up from 14.9 lakh hectares to 16.07 lakh hectares, whereas the land held by semi-medium and medium farmers have been reduced to less than 50 per cent, and in case of large farmers the total available land is negligible i.e. 2.19 lakhs hectares. Similarly, there is an increase in cultivated land by SC and ST marginal farmers. The total land operated by SC marginal farmers in 1995–96 was 5.33 lakh hectares whereas in 2000–01 it became 6.59 lakh hectares. It was 1.85 lakh hectares for ST marginal farmers in 1995–96 whereas it increased to 2.07 lakh hectares in 2000–01, whereas in case of large ST farmers, it has become nil from 530 hectares in 1995–96. Similarly, considerable reduction in area cultivated by semi-medium and medium farmers belonging to SC and ST farmers is observed. Cases of SC and STs show that the land reform measures have really benefitted the lowest strata of the society socially and economically. Even the ownership of land in case of SC and ST marginal farmers has increased. In 1995–96, 81 per cent SCs were holding land whereas in 2000–01, 85.4 per cent SC marginal farmers were landowners. In case of ST, 77.17 per cent marginal farmers were there in 1995-96, whereas in 2000–01, 80.42 per cent marginal ST were the land holders. The number of large holdings from the category of semi-medium and medium consequently have been considerably reduced. In fact, the ST large farmers have become nil. It shows that there is a peaceful revolution. This has also been reflected in increase of area cultivated by SCs and STs. In 1995–96, 48.67 per cent area was cultivated by the SCs whereas in 2000–01 the area cultivated was 60.11 per cent of arable land. So also in 1995–96, 47.4 per cent. ST population of marginal farmers cultivated land whereas in 2000–01, 52.33 per cent of STs marginal farmers cultivated the land".[2] Thus, land reform measures have created the basic stability in the rural society of West Bengal. As a result the Naxalite movement will be destabilised in West Bengal. However, there are stray movements in the State by the extremists for the following factors;

1. Discrimination by the Panchayat bodies in distribution of fruits of rural development schemes.
2. Neglect of the area being far-flung from the main stream of development.
3. Increase of awareness of rights among the neglected rural population specially STs.
4. Lack of education and lack of health facilities in these areas than other areas.
5. Non-effective participation by the ST representatives because of their simplicity in the functioning in grass roots level decision making bodies regarding rural development schemes specially Panchayats.

Tenancy distribution of land

West Bengal is the only state in the country, which has recorded about 15 lakh bargadar on about 11.1 lakh acres of land. There is hardly any recording of sharecroppers in other states. They just want to overlook the issue showing that there are actually no share-croppers, which is not a fact on the ground. "Haryana had 18.22 per cent land under tenancy in 1981–82 whereas West Bengal had only 12.34 per cent land under tenancy and Haryana has not recorded any share-cropper. Similarly, total land in UP was 10.24 per cent under tenancy as per NSS 1981–82 figures whereas the recording of sharecroppers is negligible. There is no problem if there is no tenancy like in Gujarat (1.9 per cent), Kerala (2.05 per cent). Average number of tenants in a village in West Bengal is 50, in UP it is 14 and 20 in Tamilnadu. Frequency of change of plots is almost negligible. In West Bengal 97.09 per cent tenants do not change plots whereas in UP 47 per cent tenants do not change plots. Tamilnadu is another State which shows 95.97 per cent stability of plots by tenants. In UP, the STs are not shown under tenancy whereas in West Bengal 20.3 per cent STs are tenants. It means from tenancy point of view also there is stability in rural West Bengal. On the other hand, unrecorded tenants were noticed in the villages of Bihar as 95.36 per cent, UP 87.29 per cent and Haryana 57.8 per cent"[3].

Distribution of surplus vested land

West Bengal is the leader in the country in respect of distribution of vested land. The State has distributed almost 22 per cent of the total surplus land distributed in the country to almost 53 per cent of the total beneficiaries in the country. The total beneficiaries of land distribution i.e. patta holders are 29 lakh on an area of 10.23 lakh acres as per reports published by Government of India, ministry of rural development. Similarly, land has been distributed to about 3.16 lakh poor families for homestead purpose involving a quantum of 18,989 acres of land. The above facts reveal that land reform provides basic stability in the State.

Land Reform and Productivity

It is a wrong conception that land reform is anti productivity. In fact, increase of productivity is the ultimate aim of the land reform measures. The West Bengal is an example. Due to land reform, the productivity has increased manifold and the State has now become self-sufficient in food production. The recent study by the Food and Agricultural Organization of the United Nations has found that small land holdings given by Government is creating confidence in rural masses.

"In the later phases of the land reform, the administrators began allocating the vested land in smaller parcels. Given the fact that large number of landless are owning even a very small parcel of land, this implementation of policy made good sense".

Most interviewees who commented on the relative effectiveness of the land redistribution, stated that those who had received agricultural land had realized significant livelihood improvements as a result. There were, however, some exceptions. One farmer who had not himself received land reported that households in his village who had received land had not realized significant benefits because they lacked implements and thus were not able to put the land to good use. The same farmer claimed that some of those beneficiaries had mortgaged their land away to larger farmers. A farmer in another village who had received vested land reported that while the former owner had produced three crops per year, he was only able to produce one crop per year.

Two farmers interviewed, had received homestead plots. The homestead plots allocated were extremely small, typically 0.04 acres (about 1700 square feet) or less. Even in such tiny plots, we observed that these interviewees and others who had received tiny household plots were growing vegetable or had planted fruit trees for household consumption (Rural Development Institute, Washington, USA)"[4].

When I joined as Land Reforms Commissioner, I identified the blocks affected by Naxalism in the state. After that, it was assessed how much government surplus land is available for distribution in these blocks. Then, block land and land reforms officers of these blocks along with their respective subdivisional and district land and land reforms officers were called in a meeting at the state headquarters.

During the meeting, the plan of action was drafted to distribute most of the remaining government vested lands to the really deserving landless beneficiaries irrespective of political affiliation. It was pointed out that the joint field verification of land along with the panchyat functionaries takes time. To tackle this problem, instructions were given to do field verification by government machinery only with amin and revenue inspector at the gram panchayat level. The list of proposed beneficiaries was also traditionally submitted by the panchayat functionaries. It was also changed as BPL lists were readily available at block and gram panchayat level. Out of those, landless persons were to be identified first. Priority was given to ST and SC landless BPL families or persons.

A time bound programme was chalked out and director of land records & surveys was asked to monitor the progress of work. Officers from directorate of land records and surverys were also deputed in three affected districts of West Medinapur pur, Bankura and Purulia. They were asked to visit those three districts and affected blocks to guide the field functionaries to expediate preparation of case records for final decision by the land subcommittee (Bhumi "O" Ban Sthayee Samity) of the Panchayat Samity. Final gearing up was done by fixing the patta distribution camps at selected places where dignitaries or VIPs would attend the programmes of distribution of land. The first such camp in the worst affected blocks was attended by LRC himself. This motivated the local level machinery. This also expedited the decision making by panchayat bodies and subdivisional officers who have not been attaching so much importance to the job.

One patta distribution camp was even attended by the Chief Minister himself. Other ministers including minister of land and land reforms of the Government of West Bengal attended patta distribution programmes. Senior officers attended the programme where ministers were not available. This has generated confidence among tribals and others who were feeling neglected due to apathy of their panchayat representatives who were again very simple people. They could not overcome obstacles created by the middle class bureaucracy armed with feudal rules and regulations in the rural development works. It was ensured that the deserving persons get pattas. This generated confidence and support in the masses residing in far-flung areas of the state who have become supporters of Naxalism. They came in great numbers in these camps. Wherever, lands were not available, government implemented another land distribution scheme by purchasing lands from the open market with state government funds. Rest of the things were done by departmental funds of Public Works Deptt. and 12th Finance Commission to construct roads in these inaccessible areas.

The correct message has also reached the local rural development administration including panchayat that they have to function without fear and favour. The political will also was clearly demonstrated by the top government functionaries and ministers attending to the land reforms programmes.

Land Reform vis-a-vis Naxalism

There has been considerable dilution in the ideological purity of the Left wing extremist movement and a noticeable criminalisation of its cadres at the grassroots level. As a result, many landowner organizations came into existence to militarily oppose them. And some of these violent groups have large support base including that of high castes in Bihar. Several factors have helped to sustain the LWE movement, some of which are on account of administrative lacunae. These include *inter alia* shortcomings and delays in the criminal justice system, absence of rural policing, absence of a satisfactory mechanism for instant justice in the rural areas, policy changes introduced as a result of change in government at the state level and lack of a political direction in some cases. All these factors only assist the Naxalite cause and prompt the rural poor to gravitate towards the movement. A much more comprehensive and holistic approach needs to be adopted to tackle the problem of Left wing extremism. Lack of land reforms, declining standards in the political/administrative/judicial systems and the perceived failure of the democratic process in some areas to provide an adequate channel for the people to meet their grievances are basic issues without tackling which the Left wing extremist philosophy will find increasing acceptance in several parts of the country. Thus, implementation of social legislation including land reforms, restoration of tribal lands, distribution of surplus land, minimum wages and schemes to tackle rural indebtedness need to be taken up on a priority. However, the task of providing an appropriate climate for these agencies to function will simultaneously have to be accomplished by the police.

References

[1] Agrawal, P. K. *Land Reforms in India, Constitutional and Legal Approach,* (with special reference to U.P.) published by M D Publications, Daryaganj, New Delhi.

Issues in Land Reforms, published by Rajiv Gandhi Institute for Contemporary Studies, Rajiv Gandhi Foundation, Jawahar Bhawan, New Delhi.

[2] Agricultural Census Report - 2000-01 for State of West Bengal, (summary), published by Land & Land Reforms Deptt. & Directorate of Agriculture, Govt. of W.B., Dec. 2005.

[3] Iyer, K.Gopal, *Land Reforms in India* : Volume-I, published by Land Reforms Unit, Lal Bahadur Shastri National Academy of Administration, Mussoorie.

[4] *RDI(#112) Land Reform Law and Implementation in West Bengal : Lessons and Recommendations,* published by Rural Development Institute, Scattle, Washington 98105, USA, Dec. 2001.

10

Distribution of Government Surplus Land in Uttar Pradesh

UP is the most populous state in the country. As one of the pioneer states in the field of land reforms, the Government of UP enacted the Uttar Pradesh Zamindari Abolition Act 1950 which prohibited leasing of land except in special circumstances like the disabled persons, defence services, widows and minors. As a result, the tenancy nearly came to an end. Share-cropping, of course, exists in all states of India. West Bengal recognizes it in all its aspects and about 15 lakh share-croppers have been recorded in West Bengal. Even in Bangladesh and America, share-cropping is recognized. If self-cropping is agreed to be the best alternative, let us accept that in most situations, share-cropping is the second best alternative.

With the changing times, UP revenue administration had to realize the need for change of their approach towards tenancy. In fact, in UP, the hidden share-cropping is rampant. The person who cultivates the land of another person on condition to share crop is known as bataidar, bhagdar or adhiar. In UP, there are million of instances where people are leasing out their land for cultivation. The transactions are like ordinary business transactions for a season, for a year or more. Seeing these types of cultivation in UP, one tends to support contract farming though contract farming is anti-farmer and it has to be adopted only in a limited way in a well defined conditional environment.

As per field survey done by me during 1990-92 and reflected in the book "Land Reforms in India", there are approximately 16 per cent share-croppers in Uttar Pradesh. Thus, there will be about 30.37 lakh unrecorded tenants in Uttar Pradesh out of total holdings 187.85 lakh (1981).

However, from 1981 to 1991, there was an increase of agricultural labourers to the tune of 25 lakh. This is very serious. The reason partly is that the unrecorded share-croppers are driven out of their fields and they then have no other alternative except to resort to daily labour. The average acre leased in by pure tenant is 0.61 ha.

Recording of Share-croppers in U.P.

Within the framework of existing laws, the share-croppers can be recorded in Uttar Pradesh in the following procedure :

Under Section 33-A[2] of the U.P. Land Revenue Act No. 8 of 1977, the provision has been substituted as under:

"The provisions of sub-section [1] shall *mutatis mutandis* apply to a person who has been admitted as a sirdar of any land u/s 195 of the Uttar Pradesh Zamindari Abolition and Land Reforms Act, 1950, before the commencement of the Uttar Pradesh Land Laws [Amendment] Act, 1977 or as a bhumidhar with non-transferable rights under said section after such commencement, or as an asami of any land u/s 197 of the first mentioned Act."

The State should arrange for recording of asami on a large scale as a policy as kanungo and other lower officers will not be able to face the powerful lobby of landholders in villages. This can be achieved on the same pattern as 'Barga Operation' in West Bengal. For the purpose of the programme, the State can be divided into two broad areas.

(a) Where neither K-B [Settlement and Survey] operations have been undertaken recently nor consolidation operations have been started.

(b) Where the consolidation operations and survey and settlement operations had finished long time back.

The areas under category *(a)* have to be covered under a crash-programme of "Operation Bataidar". Composite squads of the land revenue machinery and settlement department could be organized. Kanungo or any other person as per the changed designation be made its in-charge as he is legally authorized to sign the certificate of recording. A squad will work in a specified priority pocket to be selected by the settlement officer and chief revenue officer in consultation with gram panchayats/khand samiti/ zilla parishad or peasants organizations working in the area for recording u/s 33-A[2] to be accomplished within a short specified time. A methodology may be prescribed for the purpose. Each squad will preferably take up a group of mouza at a time. A meeting has to be held in the area either in the afternoon or evening whenever it is convenient for the larger number of subtenants, bataidar and agricultural labourers and asamis by issuing a general public notice. Places of habitual congregation of such persons may be selected as venues of such meetings. Meeting places should be generally near the residence of potential beneficiaries. In the evening meetings, discussions regarding rights and duties should be held partly for dissemination of information and partly for helping the poor people, asamis, bataidars and agricultural labourers, more specifically about the right of cultivation which can be ensured by recording, about the pooling of funds flowing from IRDP [Integrated Rural Development Programme], Jawahar Rozgar Yojana, NREGP [National Rural Employment Guarantee Programme], ITDP [Integrated Tribal Development Project], Prime Minister Sadak Rozgar Yojana, 100 days Rozgar Yojana [NREGP] or Area [like Hills etc] Development programmes and other Central or State Sector schemes for agricultural development and about the need for organizations of their own to secure enduring benefits either from land reform or from any other general development programme. Wholehearted cooperation should be sought from the panchayat raj institutions. Review should be regularly held at district, division and state levels. Under the provisions of Section 40[2] if the collector or the tahsildar is unable to satisfy himself as to which party is in possession, he will ascertain by summary inquiry who is the person best entitled to the property, and shall put such person in possession. This power can also be delegated to the squads during the

"Operation Bataidar" or operation u/s 33-A[2]. Similar action can also get support from provisions in Sections 48, 49 etc. In fact, record officers, have been appointed in Kaimur Range in the then Mirzapur district, now Sonbhadra district, for recording of tribals on their lands under instructions from the Supreme Court as a result of a PIL.

Distribution of Government Surplus Land

Uttar Pradesh lags behind in distribution of land. Though it is one of the largest states in the country only 2,63,225 acres of agricultural land could be distributed out of 3,39,385 acres of land available for distribution. Total number of beneficiaries are 3,03,867, whereas in West Bengal total number of beneficiaries are 28.5 lakh.

Land under litigation is about 50,000 acres. And wasteland distributed is 24.89 lakh acres as per 2006–07 report published by the ministry of rural development, Government of India in April, 2007.

There is lot of hunger for land in UP and number of agriculture labour is gradually increasing.

Many of the assignees of government-vested lands have not yet got actual possession of their land and erstwhile powerful landowners continue to get these lands cultivated by their musclemen. Encroachments should be immediately removed from their lands held by pattadars by the respective district magistrate. Some of the pattadars or AVLs have not cultivated their land because institutional finance is not available to them. As a result, they have leased out their small parcels of land to other farmers having means and resources for cultivation.

This doesn't mean that the state should encourage leasing out by these poor men. On the other hand, state should arrange crop financing to them at a concessional rate of interest (4%) so that they can cultivate their land by their own labour which is the greatest satisfaction for a villager. Contract farming can never be another alternative for these poor farmers. It will mean that the state wants to increase the number of landless persons and agricultural labourers.

According to a Chinese proverb, the number of times a farmer puts his foot on his land, production will increase. Naturally, a farmer will visit his own field . One cannot go and trespass land belonging to another person. Owning land gives so much satisfaction and security to the poor person that he puts best of his labour and attention to the land. Labour constitutes 30-40 per cent as input in agriculture. As a result, the production increases automatically. Secondly, there is no other alternative employment available to this army of unemployed persons in rural areas. There are about 27 per cent persons below poverty line even today. They require land to take benefit under some scheme or the other of the Government. Banks will not allow any credit to the persons below poverty line unless they have land which is an identification for a villager.

Out of 96.36 per cent persons found in possession of land, only 66.59 per cent were recorded in revenue records as per survey in 1992. This gap needs to be filled up immediately.

The ceiling limit for irrigated land with one crop is 10.95 ha and for irrigated crops is 7.30 ha and for dry land it is 18.25 ha. This should be reduced to 7.5 ha, 5 ha and 12 ha respectively and process of vesting should go on. After the implementation of ZA&LR Act and the UP Imposition of Ceiling on Land Holdings Act 1960, some new landlords have sprung up. They should be taken care of and equitable distribution of rural landed properties should be a continuous process to establish an egalitarian society in the state where there is so much flagrant class-discrimination and class-difference. The society has to be an integrated unit.

Exemptions of religious and charitable trust from imposition of ceiling, exemptions of groves and abadi, benami transactions, transfers by the adverse possessions, arithmetical mistake, incorrect compilation of 61-B [total landholding of a person in Uttar Pradesh], *hibba* name by muslims and problems in the definition of family, were some of the reasons behind failure of land ceiling. Complication in deciding ceiling limits for various qualities of land and defining family, leads to prolonged trail of cases, leading to higher possibility of mischief. Many people were shown 'dead' before 1973 on the basis of certificates given by Gram Pradhans. Many divorces were obtained on paper, many children were adopted and many other children were shown to be adults on the basis of 'Farzi Parivar' register. Some other provisions in ceiling law are chiefly responsible for poor availability of surplus land. These are:

a) Provision to give separate ceiling limit for major sons in the family.

b) Provision for holding land up to twice the ceiling limit for families with over five members.

c) Provision for treating every shareholder of the joint family as applicable in personal law as separate unit for ceiling limit.

d) Misclassification of land.

e) Misapplication of appropriate ceiling for land very newly irrigated by public investment, etc.

Performance of Uttar Pradesh regarding the imposition of ceiling on landholdings has not been very satisfactory. The 1960 Act could not cut much ice. So it was drastically modified in 1973. But by the time of the coming of 1972 Act, only 2.87 lakh acres out of the estimated 7.50 lakh owners have been declared surplus.

Between verbal discussions, introduction of ceiling legislation and final passing of the bill in the form of an Act, there was such time gap that people could always conveniently make nami or benami transfers of all lands above the expected ceiling, although benami and nami transfers after 24-1-71 were declared ineffective for the purpose of ceiling and mechanism was provided to detect such cases. The law provided for only filing of returns by the landowners. Since big landowners had the support of local administration, ceiling law existing only on paper was natural. Ceiling cases linger for many years. Due to delay in allotment, allottees are unable to take effective possessions over the allotted lands. Land is sometimes not allotted to deserving persons. In courts, State is represented by naib-tahsildars, who very often are not aware of the up to date position of laws and rules and also are no match to the lawyers engaged by parties in marshalling laws and evidence. Minor officials are at the mercy of influential large landowners. Land allotted is more often *usar* and *banjar*. Weaker sections are not organized and are not vocal. Supervision of senior officials is slack.

Loopholes in ceiling laws are also required to be plugged. There should be no relaxation of ceiling limit for religious or charitable trust or wakf, endowment or institution.

Conclusion

State of UP is at a critical juncture. The poor people have asserted and the new Government has been installed. State of UP had to do away with Uttarakhand because the Z.A & L.R. Act 1950 was not applied there.

Similarly, some exemptions were made in Mirzapur South District and Banaras State. Now, Naxalite agitation is raising up its head there. State owned Nazul land is also excepted. And it is a bone of contention and source of corruption. Land reform is the best solution to the problem of Naxalism which is flourishing in UP.

It is therefore, suggested that serious attention should be given to implement the twin measures of land reforms i.e. recording of sharecroppers and distribution of govt. surplus land. Political will as well as administrative will is required to implement the land reforms measures. I am sure that UP can enter into a new era of agricultural production and egalitarian society if land reform measures are properly implemented with immediate effect.

11

Land Reforms in Chhattisgarh

Chhattisgarh is a newly formed State carved out of erstwhile Madhya Pradesh consisting of seven districts namely Bilaspur, Raipur, Durg, Rajnandgaon, Raigarh, Sarguja and Bastar.

More than 80 per cent of Chhattisgarh's population live in its villages and only 12 per cent of the region's agricultural land is irrigated. The little irrigation facility that exists is limited only to the plain region. Hardly any irrigation is there in extremists' affected districts of Bastar and industrialisation has managed to engage only about 16 lakh persons in urban centres out of a total population of 1.76 crore as per 2001 census.

Thus, land reform is the central issue in Chhattisgarh which will encompass following components :

1. Distribution of land to the landless under Land Ceiling Acts and ensuring possession of lands to the allottees of the government vested land.
2. Land alienation.
3. Non-recording of sharecroppers or bataidar.
4. Land buying/grabbing by new landlords and exploitation of underground water by them.

The Chhattisgarh Mukti Morcha (CMM) under Comrade Shankar Guha Niyogi cultivated surplus land in Pithora, Basna, Saraipali areas of Raipur district. After the well-planned and conspiratorial murder of Guha Niyogi by the vested interests, the movement went into the hands of the extremists.

The tribals have faith in local moneylenders and not in banks and co-operative institutions. They are further vulnerable to exploitation because of their innate cultural ethics of honesty and morality and their concern for the present instead for the future. The alienation of land by the tribals to the non-tribals for various reasons added to their woes. The collector permitted alienation of agricultural land under the sham classification of non-agriculture land. Secondly, collector did not apply adequate force to restore their lands. The quantum of illegal (benami) land alienation from tribals to non-tribals is like that part of the iceberg that remains under the surface of water.

The fundamental cause of giving tribal land to protect the tribals can be successful only if it is complemented by measures to meet their genuine credit needs for cultivation including those for consumption and to protect them from usury. Secondly, the tribals having non-tribal lands are equally vulnerable to exploitation. The judicial redress is not available to them unless they seek joint redress or go through legal aid system.

After orders passed in favour of tribals, non-tribals should be forcibly evicted from the lands and administration should ensure peaceful and effective possession of lands to the tribals. There should be irrefutable presumption that the lands shall belong to the original tribals unless it is obtained as per provision of law with the permission of the collector.

The present legal measures to protect tribals from exploitation by money lenders should be made more stringent and proactive. Co-operative society or government body should come to the protection of the tribals to take the burden of loan and ensure him delivery of land free from all encumbrances.

As per 1992 rural census of NSS, the total area leased in came to only 7 per cent of the area owned by all households. Thus, like MP, Chhattisgarh is a low tenancy state. However, there is 25 per cent of the total area under lease. Moreover, the village-level study of LBSNAA reports that sharecropping accounts for over 75 per cent of tenants and 65 per cent of the area leased in.

There are three dominant patterns of sharecropping arrangements, which vary in incidence across regions :

1. In 30 per cent of the cases, the sharecropper has to bear the entire cost of cultivation and gets only half the share of the gross produce.
2. In 14 per cent of the cases, the sharecropper bears the entire cost of production and gets 75 per cent of the gross produce.
3. In 56 per cent of the cases, the landowner and the sharecropper share the cost and the gross produce equally.

The stagnation in agricultural productivity is of concern in the extremists' affected areas. It shows that the productivity per landowner in the agricultural sector has not increased. There is need for more investment in the agricultural sector though the size of farm has reduced and number of marginal and small farms has increased. This is possible only through institutional financing of pattadars and share croppers though not recorded even. Out of all divisions, Bilaspur division having Bastar district (undivided) has 75 per cent poverty as compared to 60 per cent in the state. The district is now divided into three districts namely Bastar, Dantewla and Kanker. The rainfall is also inadequate. It is in few strong spells and, therefore, rain off and evaporation are more. As a result in the absence of protective irrigation, the rice crop is highly prone to agricultural drought. A location specify strategy for extremists' affected areas has to be developed in Chhattisgarh. Total Watershed Planning (TWP) is one of the solutions. It will stabilise the natural resourse house so as to facilitate its equitable and long-term use. The preservation of the natural base and ecology of these is the priority area for action.

Land Records not updated

The land records regarding facts of cultivation are not updated for years. As a result, the farmers are denied access to credit, electricity or agricultural inputs and deprived of benefits of various anti-poverty programmes. The Panchayati Raj Institutions (PRIs) have to be more effective and assertive in collaboration with the local non-governmental or governmental bodies. If the vested interests in bureaucracy or elsewhere threaten them, they should face them with perseverance and sustainability. PRIs should ensure that they control Common Property Resources (CPR) like *naala* (drains), ponds, common grazing areas, outskirts of reserved forests, barren and degraded forests and even forest produce which cannot be used otherwise by the forest officials of the forest department. However, as per the latest initiative of the government, the tribals living in forest areas will be given titles and they will be entitled to use forest produce without any fear or discrimination.

However, the State must not abandon its crucial role in protecting the cause of land reforms in these backward regions simply by handing over its pious responsibilities to PRIs and NGOs.

Programme of Adhikar Abhiyan

The united MP administration started an innovative scheme known as Adhikar Abhiyan. It was to ensure the restoration of land to the dispossessed Bhumi Swamis. This ensured delivery of physical possession to patta holders and punishment to the vested interest who resisted this process. In UP, it was implemented successfully. But these campaigns are terminated before they are completed. It is to be kept in mind that land reforms is a continuous process. The tribals cannot resist temptation to alienate land or mortgage the same because of their pressing personal, family or social obligations. If such processes are implemented on a certain intervals, then the villagers will find it a financial folly to mortgage the land of the tribals and the tribals on the other hand will take shelter of the government or semi-government institutions, like banks, cooperative societies and others who will at least not exploit them to that extent.

Salwa Judum

'Official' version of the Salwa Judum portrays it as a people's struggle against the excesses of Naxalism. Villagers go into other villages and convince them to join. Many are attracted to join by the promise of payment of Rs.1,500 per month, the weapon and the hope of getting permanent employment in the police force. But due to retaliatory action by the Maoists to and mismanagement on the part of police administration, nearly 46,000 people were living in camps in abysmal conditions which the villagers do not like. They were to be settled in 581 new villages near roadside but the scheme could not get off the ground. Both sides claim civilian deaths. The government officers list 268 civilians killed (including some 50 SPOs) and 706 injured by the Maoists since June 2005, the Maoists have released a partial list of 116 civilians killed by the Salwa Judum till March 2006. In addition 72 police personnel and 30 Naxalites have died.

The leader of the Salwa Judum, Mahendra Karma told that it was the 'citizens' initiative' on the pattern of. 'Bhumkal', the rebellion against the British, because the Maoists had singularly opposed modern development.

The Maoists claim to include 60 lakh people in their 'organisation sweep' of their Dandakaranya "guerrilla zone" (comprising Godchiroli, Bhandara, Bala Ghata, Rajnandgaon undivided Bastar and Malkangiri). Maoist literature claims that they have engaged considerably in development work over the last 20 years. For instance, in South Bastar and Godchiroli, they have established 135 people's clinics, started 6 primary schools, 10 night schools, built 25 huts for government teachers to persuade them to attend schools regularly, set up 10 village libraries, 81 tanks, four lakh fish seedlings, bullock carts built in 10 villages, diesel pump sets introduced in 9 villages, 268 cattle detention yards built, 5 rice mills introduced, people trained in forest protection, cooperative paddy bank set up and agricultural cooperatives created in 220 villages.

However, in its drive to establish their own 'Janata Sarkar', the Maoists have resisted even genuine government initiatives. The Maoists are dependent on contractors for funds and the contractors are dependant on Maoists for work in their areas.

Whatever may be the reality, the Salwa Judum campaigning brings out the fact that the Maoists' movement is not beyond public scrutiny. If they fail or go astray, another countervailing movement will arise and resist in their own courtyard. Thus, the Maoists have to be very cautious. Had they attended only to implementation of land reforms, their movement could have gone unchallenged. The Government machinery is better equipped in doing developmental works and have unlimited recourses. This is high time that the Government implements land reform measures without further delay in Chhattisgarh where the Maoists have lost focus of their main aim. However, in the democratic system like ours, violence neither by the Maoists nor by the Salwa Judum can be justified. A third path has to be carved out, sooner or later.

12

Land Reform Measures in Madhya Pradesh

Madhya Pradesh had about 6 crore population as per 2001 census. The scheduled tribe population is 1.22 crore which is 20.3 per cent of the state's population and scheduled caste population is 15.17 per cent. Madhya Pradesh is rich in forests. Tribals and forests are inseparable. Most of the tribals inhabit forest areas or the fringes of the forests. There are 14 forest rich districts which are inhabited by almost 80 per cent of the tribal population. Madhya Pradesh has 20 per cent of the total forest cover in the country.

The districts which are mostly affected by the Naxalite activities are forest rich districts like Balaghat and Mandla. Mandla district has the famous Kanha National Park. Similarly, some portion of Jabalpur district covering forest rich areas is also affected by the Naxal activities. The villages covered by Naxalites are located in dense forest areas where the communication and transportation facilities are very poor. The Gond and Baiga people of these villages used to go for bamboo cutting and other work to Chandrapur district of Maharashtra and Bastar district (now Chhattisgarh) where they came in touch with the Naxalites who were active there. Secondly, the economy of the tribal areas cannot be thought of without forests. Therefore, in Madhya Pradesh, we shall examine the Naxalism vis-a-vis forest management and how can forest management be made supportive to the tribal economy which will also be consistent with the preservation and maintenance of forests.

The social forestry failed in Madhya Pradesh so also farm forestry. However, joint forest management (JFM) was to some extent successful with its 'care and share philosophy'. Fulfilment of livelihood needs of the poor and the tribals are the preconditions for the sustainability of natural resources. Therefore, the tribals will like and encourage 'trees of poor' which are essentially employment generating trees, as they require labour for gathering and collection, as opposed to trees which are clear-felled and either fill up government coffers or the bellies of the rich or forest mafia. The tribals worship such trees which help to sustain their livelihood needs. Therefore, in Madhya Pradesh land reforms will have another component of forest. This will also be applicable in other Naxalite areas which are forest and tribal dominated. This is borne by the fact that over 60 per cent of the country's forest cover is found in 187 tribal districts of India where less than eight per cent of national population lives.

Rather than going into theoretical aspect of tribal vis-a-vis forest, let us examine how the recently passed "the Scheduled Tribes and other Traditional Forest Dwellers (Recognition of Forest Rights) Act 2006 by Parliament can change the outlook of the tribals towards development. The Act was a long time need. It was implemented in bits and pieces in various parts of the country through executive orders but a consolidated Act was not passed. This may be termed as a *magna carta* in the field of forest management, protecting the interest of the tribals if the Act is implemented with speed and in true spirit.

The Act aims "to recognize and vest the forest rights and occupation in forest land in forest dwelling Scheduled Tribes and other traditional forest dwellers who have been residing in such forests for generations but whose rights could not be recorded..."

In the Preamble of the Act, the state has accepted that "their forest rights on ancestral lands and their habitat were not adequately recognized in the consolidation of state forests during the colonial period as well as in independent India resulting in historical injustice to the forest dwelling Scheduled Tribes and other traditional forest dwellers who are integral to the very survival, sustainability of the forest ecosystem".

Tribals have emotional, psychological and cultural attachments with the forest and they always live in the forest so also Naxalites. On the other hand, for non-tribal forest dwellers, forest related livelihood activities are the last resort. However, the Act cannot discriminate. The Act in most of the states is being administered by the tribal department or the backward class department who are working for the tribals and other backward classes like scheduled castes.

The following problems are coming in the way of implementation of the provisions of the Act before the tribals can be handed over records-of-rights for lands in forests or fringes of the forests;

1. The tribals do not have proper caste certificates. Issuance of caste or tribe certificate is a Herculean job which is not possible for the simple and illiterate tribal to get from the respective subdivisional officer.
2. The revenue machinery is not prepared to take up the responsibility of such a stupendous job of survey of all tribal areas near forests, the demarcation of land of each tribal or dweller and prepare a record-of-rights for each individual raiyat or owner.
3. The forest officials without whose co-operation the Act cannot take off, are not mentally prepared to accept the primary position accorded to the tribals whom they used to treat like thieves or trespassers in the forests.
4. In some of the areas Gram Sabhas are not constituted or convened. Then how can the cases be cleared, remains to be answered
5. The Act is silent against lot of charges/prosecutions pending against the tribals under the Forest Conservation Act 1980 and the Indian Forest Act 1927 with retrospective effect.

There is no provision in the Act of 2006 that cases under the Forest Conservation Act 1980 against the forest dwelling scheduled tribes for accessing minor forest produce would be dropped or closed. There are thousands of such cases pending and hundreds of plough and cattle remain impounded by the forest department officials. These cases are to be dropped or withdrawn by the Government.

There were 2,57,226 forest cases pending against 1,62,692 tribals between 1953 and 30th June 2004 under Sections 26,33 and 41 of the Indian Forest Act 1927 pertaining primarily to illegal felling of trees for domestic use and ferrying of wood by bullock carts in Chhattisgarh as on 8 Nov. 2005 and 2531 such cases in Orissa as on 10th March 2005. Thus, incidents of the high handedness is more in the state of Chhattisgarh. As a result, proportionate influence of the Naxalism is more in the state of Chhattisgarh. If the administration terms its majority population as accused persons or criminals, they will have to behave accordingly under whatever guise it may be.

The same problems were projected on 25th June 2008 in a seminar convened by the Ekta Parishad attended *inter alia* by Chief Minister Shivraj Singh Chauhan, principal secretary, scheduled tribes welfare department, principal secretary, forest department and other service officers. It was alleged that the forest officials were not accepting the applications for recording their names because the tribals have been encroaching upon the forest lands for a long time. Thus, the Act has yet to be popularized through wide publicity and training so that even the lowest level functionaries recognize the legal position.

There were large scale transfers of tribal lands to the non-tribals. Even forest department got transferred about 1 lakh acres of tribal land through tribal agriculture societies. In districts of Gwalior and Morena, lot of Bhoodan lands have been transferred.

The Status of alienation and restoration of Tribal Land

As per Government of India's department of land resources, ministry of rural development report, the position as on September 2008 was as below including Chhattisgarh.

- No. of cases filed in Courts—53,806
  Area 1,58,398 acres
- Cases disposed of by the Courts—29,596
  Area 97,123 acres
- Cases decided in favour of tribals—21,834
  Area 67,862 acres

- Cases in which land was restored to tribals—21,834
  Area 67862 acres
- Cases pending in Courts—24,210
  Area 61,275 acres

The cases pending are huge involving 61275 acres. These are either in revenue courts or with officers under the tribal department. A special drive and fixing up of responsibility for non-disposal or delay in disposal can ease out the situation. Cases rejected against the tribals should be re-examined by superior officer or group of superior officers. Responsibility should be fixed for rejection or disposal of cases against the poor tribals. Appeals or review in suitable cases should be filed. The revenue courts should follow the dictum of the latest amendment in the Code of Civil Procedure (Order XVII Rule-I), wherein not more than three adjournments should be granted in any case. Rules should be framed by the Government of MP so as not to allow more than three adjournments in a case of restoration of land to the tribal. More officers should be deputed for this purpose exclusively. The courts should also ensure that the tribals are given possession of the land simultaneously and the other person is paid due compensation on behalf of the government.

As regards Bhoodan lands, 31,000 acres of land is still to be distributed in addition to 92,000 acres available under land ceiling surplus land which is of good quality cultivable agriculture land.

Madhya Pradesh government has hardly done anything on the distribution front of government wastelands and is one of the lowest in the country though the State has the largest geographical area in the country. Only 79,000 acres of land has been distributed by September 2006 though the State has 57,134 sq km. as per report of the Government of India which is 18.53% of the total land 3,08,252 sq km. The Government of MP should awake and do the needful *inter alia* to distribute government wasteland among the landless persons giving priority to the tribals.

1. The tribal land is alienated through transfers or transfers by concealing material facts which are not allowed and should be prohibited by way of new amendment in the relevant Act or Acts.

2. Transfer of tribal land by the competent authorities mistakenly or by obtaining the permission by fraud should be reviewed and *suo motu* case on an application by the tribal or on his behalf by the official of scheduled tribe department or gram panchayat or panchayat samity.
3. In Scheduled areas having 50% or more than 50% scheduled tribe population, the industry using local resources and land, should not hold more than 50% shares. The government should hold more than 50% shares or holding in the company so that long term interests of the tribals can be safeguarded and they don't become foreigners in their own village.
4. The provision of conversion or diversion of agricultural land for non-agricultural purposes must be done strictly before the transfer or land acquisition so that tribals get partial advantage of enhancement of rate of land on this basis.
5. The land records should be updated in tribal pockets on priority basis and gram panchayats may be authorized to appear on behalf of the tribal to certify occupation if the tribal raiyats or land holder doesn't appear during Khanapur-Bujharat operation or later on during hearing before the survey and settlement authorities.
6. The Bhoodan lands, government waste land, Gaon sabha lands/poramboka lands have been encroached upon by the powerful landowners. They should be evicted and such lands should be distributed to the tribals and other weaker sections of the society.
7. The unirrigated or otherwise banjar lands distributed to the tribal beneficiaries should be provided with irrigation facilities or the land should be reclaimed or developed under various schemes of the rural development ministry like 100 days labour employment scheme known as NAREGA or various schemes under Integrated Tribal Development Programme (ITDP)

---

*1 sq.km. = 247 acres = 100 hectare

where lot of surplus funds go back to the Government of India as unutilized. The popularly known 100 days employment scheme has the biggest contribution to increase the daily wages in tribal areas which are starting from Rs. 35 per day. Thus, government schemes have salutary contribution which should be exploited and these schemes should be properly and honestly implemented.

8. As regards implementation of the Scheduled Tribes and other Traditional Forest Dwellers (Recognition of Forest Rights) Act 2006 now known as STORFA, the implementation is tardy. It is a stupendous task. The same revenue machinery has to take the leadership. The forest officials can not have change in their mindset by admitting a basic change in the relationship of the community and the forest. The tribals in forest fringes are not only merely the users of the forest but are also the protector albeit in association with the State. Thus, the gaps in the main Act are to be filled in by clearly spelling out their revised role in the Rules in keeping with the spirit of the new provisions. The Act should not stumble just because gram sabhas are not constituted or there are other new hindrances created. The problem should be overcome by way of envisaging foolproof administrative procedures or constituting committees having representatives from the panchayati raj institutions (PRIs) specially from the panchayat samity level or gram panchayat.
9. The gram sabha is vague. It should be gram panchayat of the gram sabha. Secondly, effective functional committee is at the panchayat samity level which is missed in the Act. This gap should be filled in.
10. The ownership of Minor Forest Produce has been unequally provided in PESA in 1996 and also in STORFA. This proposition has been pursued variously in different states ever since the consensus reached in State Ministers Conference in 1976 as a part of tribal sub plan strategy.

11. The remaining tribal lands alienated should be restored on war footing through special drive or operation like administrative mechanism.

It is hoped that Naxalism will be fully brought under control if foregoing analysis regarding tribal lands is taken into consideration and adequate measures are taken to plug loopholes in land laws specially relating to tribals.

13

Jharkhand:

A Cradle of Naxalite Movement

If any state that can be said to be fully afflicted with Naxalism, it is Jharkhand—the newly formed State from the erstwhile united Bihar. The solution regarding Naxalite problem in Bihar, *mutatis muntandis,* will apply to Jharkhand State. In fact, most of the problems of Jharkhand have been inherited by the nascent State from Bihar.

Following are generally accepted suggestions on implementation of land reforms in Jharkhand which is an important tool to tackle Naxalite problem.

1. All party consensuses should be arrived at for speeding up the implementation process of land reforms at the village level before the situation goes out of control.
2. Infrastructure should be strengthened.
3. Farmer's pass book be issued.
4. There should be regular arrangement of training of administrative personnel, concurrent evaluation of the quality of implementation and carrying out research is also recognized.
5. Correct and up-to-date records-of-rights are crucial for the implementation of land reforms. Therefore, wherever the records are incorrect and not up-to-date, necessary steps should be taken to rectify and update them.
6. For hill areas which have not been cadastrally surveyed so far, a special programme for a cadastral survey will have to be initiated.

7. Apart from the normal survey and settlement operations, which may continue where they are already under way, a record of tenants, including share-croppers and others in cultivating land, possession of the land, and having presumptive evidentiary value should be prepared for all the villages in the course of a year and the records should be maintained by annual revision. This can be done by way of digitization of village maps through computers and integrating the village map with the individual plot of record-of-segment of each saryat and updating of land records by engaging private vendors on computers where latest changes by way of mutation and conversion of lands are invariably incorporated.

8. A crash programme of recording tenants or bataidars should be undertaken on the pattern of recording of bargadars in West Bengal.

9. The tenant who is not tilling the land himself should be given an option, within a specified time, whether he would continue to cultivate the land himself.

10. Benami transfers must be declared illegal, and such transfers made in the past should be annulled and the land is vested in the government. There should be some specific provision in the tenancy laws to precisely define and describe benami transactions.

11. The existing ceiling laws should be translated into the vernacular using simple language so that all concerned have a clear understanding of the implication of the laws. Awareness, particularly amongst the beneficiaries, should be created by disseminating correct information through the audiovisual mass media.

12. Ledgers of landholdings districtwise and talukwise need to be prepared by the method of card indexing for effective implementation of ceiling laws.

13. Lists of big rural families should be drawn up at the sub-divisional level and vigorous application of the laws initiated.

14. To restore confidence among the tribals, the pending cases of all those who have been illegally dispossessed or evicted should be disposed of expeditiously by summary trials in a time bound programme. If necessary, additional special officers may also be deputed for the purpose.

15. Cases which have been suppressed due to collusion with the staff should be examined as laid down in the Act and followed up. If necessary, additional staff may be given. The onus of proving any right over the land which a non-tribal claims must be that of the claimant.

16. The tribal welfare department staff should be posted in each halka and may be utilized to identify cases of alienation and indebtedness. The welfare staff should also pursue the cases of restoration and collusive title suits and take the follow-up action to give effect to the court's decision in case of tribals.

17. People's participation in land reform measures can be ensured through a committee constituted by nominated/elected representatives from amongst the members of the scheduled tribes living in that area or through sub-committees of panchayat samitis. Such committees should be formed at the halka and/or block level for the sole purpose of implementing the aforesaid measures and should be active.

18. The classification of land in Jharkhand should be reduced to three (against the existing six):

    - irrigated,
    - unirrigated, and
    - inferior quality of land e.g., unproductive, hilly, mountainous, sandy etc.

    The ceiling for these three categories of land can be 15, 22.5 and 30 acres respectively. However, to provide incentive to farmers to improve productivity, classification of land may not be changed when private irrigation is introduced. Provisions in any case exist for refixation of ceiling if public irrigation is introduced.

19. The West Bengal Land Reforms Act 1955 as amended up to 1972, besides providing ceiling for a 'Family' unit, puts a limit for a sole surviving adult unmarried person to half of a family unit. An amendment on the West Bengal lines would facilitate effective implementation in Jharkhand.
20. The exemption granted in favour of sugar mills should be withdrawn.
21. There should be regular training of officers in order to equip them with the requisite knowledge of the laws, rules, regulations and various instructions issued by the government from time to time relating to land reforms. They should also be properly and adequately equipped with necessary skills and attitudes required for the job.
22. Section 40 should be suitably amended to prohibit any transfer of land by a member of the STs to a non-tribal.
23. A time-limit should be prescribed for every settlement operation. Departmental proceedings should be initiated against officers not conforming to these schedules, and punishment imposed.
24. The survey officials should not be allowed to open khatas in respect of such lands in the name of non-tribals which have been recorded in the name of tribal in the previous survey.
25. The government should take a lead in establishing bank/ consumption loan or micro financing scheme for the tribals in the area at the rate of not more than four per cent on the lines of the Gramin Bank Scheme in Bangladesh and the mobile banks in Pakistan.
26. There should be a major thrust on small and medium irrigation projects in these areas which are ideally suited in terms of employment potential and for the management of the cost-benefit ratio. The water resources thus created should be utilized for intensive vegetable cultivation and pisciculture.

14

Land Reforms in Bihar:

Roadblocks

There is plenty of scope to improve things in the area of land reforms in the State. If the records-of-rights are updated in Bihar and are published, many of the genuine grounds of Naxalism in Bihar can be obliterated. The status of main component of land reforms in Bihar including Jharkhand i.e. vesting of ceiling surplus land and its distribution among the beneficiaries is as follows as on 30th September 2006 (in acres).

Area declared surplus	Area taken possession	Area distributed to individual beneficiaries	Total no. of beneficiaries
4,15,447	3,90,752	3,06,964	3,79,528

SC Beneficiaries		ST Beneficiaries		Other Beneficiaries	
No.	Area	No.	Area	No.	Area
2,34,861	1,02,045	43,050	39,978	1,01,617	84,941

Distribution of Bhoodan Land upto November 2005

Area (in acres)		
Donated	Distributed	Balance
3,57,000	2,01,000	1,56,000

Distribution of Government Wastelands

Area distributed as in July, 97 (Govt. of India figures): 13,21,000

The problems were many. The information about the total land including those in benami names with the ex-zamindars is not statistically available. Besides Zamindars succeeded in keeping 14 per cent of their estate in the form of khas possession which nobody could touch. As per estimates of the state revenue department the total land in khas possession of the ex-zamindars would be to the tune of 15 lakh acres.

In addition using unscrupulous methods, such as *benamadari*, collusion with revenue officials and politicians, coupled with their social status and power, the ex-zamindars of Bihar succeeded, by and large, in protecting their class interests. The examples are there for everybody to see. The ex-zamindars of Darbhanga, Hathwa, Dumraon and Ramgarh still own large tracts of lands. Even tenure holders under them, like Raghubans Narain Singh of Kursela, happens to be a big landowner. Maul Babu who once prided himself of being a modest *raiyat* of Raj Darbhanga, now possesses around 18,000 acres of land and an airstrip!

It is clear that Bihar is lagging much behind in vesting of surplus land. In West Bengal, 13,98,139 acres of land has vested to the State though the total area of West Bengal is half of Bihar (Bihar 1,73,877 sq km, West Bengal 88.752 sq km).

In Bihar scheduled tribe population as per 2001 census is 78,45,000 which is 10% of India. In West Bengal 5,36,912 tribals got land as pattader whereas in Bihar only 43,050 tribals got government land. This is the quantum of problem in Bihar and Jharkhand which are witnessing large scale extremists' activities. On the other hand, out of 86,291 cases filed for restoration of alienated land of tribals, only about 50% cases i.e. 44,634 have gone in favour of the tribals.

However, there is still lot of scope to distribute the remaining government land and 1.56 lakh acres of Bhoodan land among the tribals on priority apart from government wasteland which is yet to be distributed. Even consolidation of land holdings of 96.05 lakh acres of land was tilted in favour of landowners. Therefore, it was stopped from 1992. It is not understood why the consolidation operation had started once again in Bihar w.e.f. 15.03.2004 without streamlining revenue administration.

The second biggest bottleneck in land reforms measure is non-recognition of sharecroppers in Bihar. As per report of Government of India as in September 2006, total number of tenants conferred ownership rights were not reported. West Bengal achieved magical feat by recording 15 lakh Borgaders or share-croppers without conferring ownership right on them. They only share 50% produce if the owner gives plough, cattle seeds, manures fertilizers and other inputs. If the sharecropper provides all inputs for cultivation, he would get 75% share of produce. The latter is only on paper but the right is there. If West Bengal can do it, why not the adjoining State of Bihar having the same system of land records and system of permanent settlement. Only little more initiative and political will are required for this purpose.

The landowners are tactfully utilising judicial proceedings to deny rights to the poor cultivators and are taking undue advantage of the corrupt and demoralised revenue machinery. They even go to West Bengal and take same order of stay or injunction on the pretext of title suit and prolong suits for years. As a result, the poor cultivators lay down their arms and hearts and leave everything on destiny. For past few years, they have now started taking recourse of naxalite elements who protect them from undue exploitation and injustice and gain revenge on the zamindars by way of armed attacks for their annihilation. The landowners have also organised themselves. Therefore, it is no longer a one way running over the others. It is only violence which comes on surface in which police and administration are dragged as law and order maintenance agency. Then, the movement of Left Wing extremists (LWE) get diverted towards the police force and their main focus is lost. It is violence, murder and forceful occupation of land all-round and no permanent solutions come forth. The lands which were once forcibly taken possession by the LWE, are recaptured by the landowner with the help of police force as the law of land is in their favour. Thus, correction and updating of land records become very crucial in Bihar for launching land reform measures. Let us examine how best the old and outdated records-of-rights in Bihar can be updated.

Combining Khanapuri with attestation and disposal of objections

Khanapuri (filling up the records) is the most critical stage in the survey operations. The rest of the stages involve correction of the database created. The matter of creating record should not be left to the amins. From the initial stage, the revenue officer or Naib Tehsildar can be associated with this work so that at later stages of attestation and objections, there may not be many objections. At initial stage, there should be transparency. Even the representatives of PRIs, should be given notice to be present. The objection should be decided at the Khanapuri attestation stage and only objections after final publication should be invited. Three stages of objections thus should be reduced to two only or even one.

Adherence to the Time frame

The total time envisaged is of two years at the maximum for survey operation in a medium sized district. Adequate number of teams should be formed even from other districts. Any operation running beyond the time frame would necessarily invite lot of complications for cost, quality and corruption will creep in. Time is a critical factor and incentives and disincentives have to be linked in order to achieve the requisite efficiency. Even some trained personnel in survey from open market may be recruited on daily wages or contract basis subject to penal disincentives for wrong or faulty recording.

Final Publication

The final publication of records should be made available in the form of Khatian to the interest holder on whatever high fee that may be decided. After a time of 60 days, the objections should be closed and final records-of-rights may be entered in revenue records on computers after disposal of all objections after giving proper opportunity of hearing to the objectors and passing reasoned orders. With the incorporations of these modifications, the records-of-rights should be finalised.

Training of Survey Personnel

There is no substitute of field survey. Unless field survey is done periodically say after every 10 years or 15 years, the computers cannot themselves correct records. Even correction of record of one landholder cannot be done because overall boundary of the village has to be tallied. This takes time. For this stupendous work, survey knowing or trained personnel are required who are in short supply. Survey institutes are closing down one by one because the revenue department is a low cost department and they can't sustain financially nowadays. Government should come in a big way to open survey institutes or survey training in ITIs or polytechnics in India. The survey work should be made little more interesting and scientific. Survey of India has expertise and is experimenting with new technologies like aerial survey but they are not able to give records-of-rights as required or used by the public in general from time immemorial.

Now, the survey personnel have to be trained in computerization of records and digitisation of maps. Then there will be constant correction of records by the same agency who will be well conversant with the field situation. Experiments of West Bengal combining management revenue functionaries and survey functionaries has also not been successful due to public pressure on management functions like correction of records, hearing of cases, mutation and conversion. As a result, the work of survey and preparation of record-of-rights terribly suffers. District collector should be strictly instructed not to engage survey and settlement staff and officers for other administrative works including elections.

Requirement of additional staff and officers

The survey and settlement wing is inadequately staffed. In West Bengal, there are 30,000 employees and officers whereas in Bihar, there will not be more than 10,000 staff and officers. The Government of India is providing liberal grants for the purpose but the State Government has to carry on the burden with its own resources. But this is worth. This is the basic responsibility of the State Government which they should discharge if they have to stay in seat of power otherwise disgruntled public led by the extremists will run over their ivory towers.

Digitization of Maps

The biggest challenge of digitisation of maps has been met and a software has been developed after toil and continuous meditation for about 15 years. In West Bengal, maps are being digitised to the accuracy of more than 99%. This will solve problem of delay of number of years in printing of maps which are integrated parts of records-of-rights. State like Bihar can employ National Informatic Centre (NIC) wing of Government of India for this purpose with success.

Ideal Records as reality

Andhra Pradesh has shown that the registration wing of government can be linked with the record of revenue or land reform wing as in West Bengal. No registration should be done unless the records are seen as correct on computer. After registration the records can be simultaneously corrected. Thus, there will be automatic system of updation of records-of-rights. The fees for mutation and conversion can be duly charged at the common service centre as done in Madhya Pradesh, Andhra Pradesh, West Bengal and Karnataka.

Once the maps are digitised, the raiyat can be given his records-of-rights along with map of plot boundaries with respect to the village. This will be the best and the final records-of-rights which will have no lacuna or gap. This record-of-rights will have all good qualities of permanent settlement in the Eastern India and North India and record with map of plot in Raiyat wari settlement in South India. The 'recording of rights' operation should be conducted in the mission approach on the pattern of 'Operation Barga 'in West Bengal.

Legal Measures

Under Section 44 of the present Bihar Land Ceiling Act, it should be obligatory for the state government to prepare and publish a record-of-rights. Therefore, instead of the word 'may', the word 'shall' should be substituted in that section. This will provide a legal basis for annual updating of records which should be done on regular basis.

The provision of consultation with landlord for subletting the land should be done away with because it practically amounts to giving the landlord the right to change his tenants.

The implementation of the Maintenance of Land Records Act 1973 should be taken up in the right earnest in blocks affected by ceiling legislation.

The laws relating to land reforms should be codified in one single statute.

The names of encroachers should not be recorded.

Administrative Measures

A separate machinery for implementing land reforms should be set up and selected officers may be put on the job.

There should be regular training of officers in order to equip them with the requisite knowledge of the law, rules, regulations and various instructions issued by the government from time to time.

Executive instructions should be reiterated so that the Police officers should be bound to follow the orders of the revenue authorities in these matters and assert their authority in the interests of the allottees of the surplus land and the bataidars or share-croppers.

Construction of the office-cum-residences for lower revenue functionaries in the tolas of the weaker sections of society will instil greater confidence and bring justice to their doorstep.

The provision of Section 71(a) of the Chhota Nagpur Tenancy Act (CNT Act) should be enforced strictly so that lands belonging to the members of the tribal community may be restored to them.

The number of appeals and revisions should be restricted to just one in order to avoid vexatious litigation.

Field visit by the original court should be made a mandatory provision in all restoration cases. Restoration register along with supporting records should be maintained at halka/Anchal/sub-divisional level.

A time limit should be prescribed for all recording operations, say one year.

A 'rakma-milan' with the previous survey should be rigidly adhered to so that the alienation of tribal land is not regularised.

The recording officer should not be allowed to open khatas in respect of such lands in the name of non-tribals which have been recorded in the name of tribals in the previous survey.

Annual computation sheets (rent-rolls) should be regularly prepared and updated.

Officers who have already done their district tenure, should be posted as settlement officers in those areas.

There should be special squad at the disposal of the deputy commissioner/district magistrate for giving possession of land to the tribals and the landless.

Bandyopadhyay Commission on Land Reforms

Government of Bihar had set up a three man commission chaired by Shri D. Bandyopadhyay who had spearheaded barga recording operation in West Bengal. It is learnt that the Commission has given its report which *inter alia* contains recommendations on strengthening administration of land revenue set-up, updating and computerisation of land records and recording of informal tenants or sharecroppers. The Government is still examining the report though Maoists have resumed agitations to implement the report.

15

Protection of Land Rights of Tribals in Orissa

Orissa was known as Kalinga in ancient times. Now, it is widely known as the land of Lord Jagannath. It has 3.7 crore population as per 2001 census (approx). It has 81,45 lakh scheduled tribe population which is 22.13 per cent of the total population which is much more than the national average of 8.2 per cent of scheduled tribe population in the country. About 75 per cent of people in Orissa depend on agriculture. Eighty per cent of these 75 per cent people are marginal farmers having less than five acres of land.

Therefore, any land reform measure to be undertaken in Orissa will have to take into account these poor tribals. Another problem in Orissa is the large scale displacement of the people due to mining projects, plantations, proposed setting up of large industries and rich farmers occupying lands of large number of poor people. As per estimate by the Ekta Parishad, an NGO, about 1.5 lakh people have been driven away from their lands and forests.

It is also a fact that the tribal belts of Andhra Pradesh, Orissa, Chhattisgarh, Jharkhand and even West Bengal where the Naxalites are most active, are also among the areas in the country that have the lowest development indicators. There have been maximum deaths due to hunger in Orissa in districts like Kashipur, Lanjigarh and Kalahandi. Kalahandi is synonymous with deaths due to hunger in the country. Of course, their level of health, literacy and housing is much lower than their counterparts in Orissa and in other parts of the country.

It is a commonly acknowledged fact that the scheduled castes now termed as dalits and tribals are the most disadvantaged sections of the Indian society. The increasing presence of Naxalites in areas dominated by adivasis has geographical reason namely that the hills and forests of Central India or earlier known as Dandakaranya are well suited to the methods of roaming guerilla warfare. But it also has a historical reason namely, that the adivasis have gained the least and lost the most from 60 years of political independence. There were local leaders from the tribals but after modern education or rising above their own clan equal or higher than general class, they got alienated from their own tribal clan. Secondly, being tradition bound, less literate or educated and having simple life style, the tribals did not even exert their rights at the panchayat levels where they could easily extra lot of benefits or gains of the development process. The present development process is demand based. Unless the baby cries, none cares for it. None goes to the doorstep of a person who is in need of help. The needy has to go for help. As a result, the tribals are left behind in the race of development though lot of funds flow for them. They live on their destiny or some so called champion of their welfare.

Status of implementation of land reforms in Orissa

(A) Implementation of land ceiling laws upto December, 2007 (GOI Report)

Returns			Area declared surplus	Area taken possession	Area distributed to individual	Total No. of beneficiaries	SC/ST beneficiaries			
Filed	Disposed	Pending					SC Beneficiaries		ST Beneficiaries	
							No	Area	No	Area
60335	60076	259	189979	171463	159546	142959	48866	51136	53060	66303

Other Beneficiaries		Area Declared Surplus but not distributed	Total Cases and Area involved in Litigation		Revenue Courts		High Courts		Supreme Court	
No.	Area	Area	Area Involved	No. of Cases	Area	No.	Area	No.	Area	No.
41033	42094	29784	15051	288	7137	169	7014	116	123	3

Area not available for distribution			Total Area not available for distribution	Net Area available for distribution
Reserved/ Transferred for public purpose	Unifit for cultivation	Misc. reasons		
5025	2539	10061	27524	1889

Bhoodan Land

Area		
Donated	Distributed	
6.39	5.80	0.59

Government Waste Land

Area Distributed in Lakh Acres	Number of Beneficiaries
7.34	NR

Alienation and Restoration of Tribal Lands

No. of cases filed in the Courts	Area	Cases disposed of by the Courts	Area	Cases rejected	Area	Cases decided in favour of Tribals	Area	Cases in which land was restored to Tribals	Area	Cases pending in Court	Area
105491	104742	104644	103556	43213	46677	61431	56879	61364	56854	847	1186

The track record of distribution of ceiling surplus land by Orissa Government seems to be satisfactory. However, one fails to understand why 5025 acres of land has been reserved for public purpose which is not in any other state. Secondly, 10,061 acres of land has not been distributed due to miscellaneous reasons or due to undisclosed reasons. Even land unfit for distribution viz. 2539 acres can be put for distribution. If the beneficiaries return or reject the land, then only it should be treated as unfit. Thus apart from 15051 acres of land locked in litigation, about 17,500 acres can be additionally put to distribution in addition to other areas of land available for distribution under Bhoodan land and the Government waste land.

It is learnt that thousands of acres of land is with Shri Jagannathji Religious & Charitable Trust spread over in all districts. As this is a government managed trust, the cultivators of the land may be recorded as sharecroppers and they may be asked to give at least 25 per cent share to the Trust if the Trust provides no input for cultivation. But this land can not be left uncared for. This should not in any case go into the hands of big landowners.

The poor people are closer to God. Let them honestly cultivate the land and offer due share to Lord Jagannath. The Trust will have to undertake extensive land reform measures.

The worrisome point is that the land of tribal landowners is not vested to government. This can not be the approach except in the North-Eastern States where community ownership is recognized as far as land of the tribal raiyats is concerned. The Government of Orissa is in the mainstream of the national life. They may make an amendment that the surplus land of the tribal landowners can only be distributed among the tribal beneficiaries. It will serve both ways and will balance the traditional and modern outlook towards landlessness among the tribals. Secondly, the land locked cases of restoration of tribal lands amounting to 4500 acres should also be decided fast. Mostly the cultivable land of the scheduled castes and scheduled tribes are unrecorded. In many cases, land owned by the tribals is physically occupied and cultivated by non-tribals. Due to ignorance and lack of awareness of land laws, the tribals accept the claim over their land by the local dominant non-tribals.

The next plank of land reform is conferment of right of cultivation or ownership on tenants.

In Orissa, 2.97 lakh tenants have been conferred ownership on 1.15 lakh acres of land, as in September 2006. This figure can also go up to a large extent as informal tenancy is in vogue in Orissa.

The Orissa Estate Abolition Act 1951, aimed at abolition of all intermediary interests including mortgages and lessees of such lands. The Orissa Estate Abolition (Amendment) Act 1972 was further enacted to extinguish outstanding estates.

But the implementation of land reform laws could not be successful due to sway of landowner class in the politics and in bureaucracy. As a result, the toiling masses in Orissa still migrate to other states in India as they do not have requisite quantum of land to hold on in their villages.

After observing the success of land reforms in the neighbouring State of West Bengal, efforts were made by government from time to time to record sharecroppers or to distribute land among the landless persons, but in the final analysis proper impact could not be seen.

Thus, the State of Orissa requires thorough review of land reform laws so that they can be implemented by the enlightened bureaucracy. The panchayat institutions are also weak in Orissa. Unless, the rural landless persons or sharecroppers are organized, no fruitful results can come out. The Panchayat bodies are also to be made truly representatives and should be protected from the onslaught of the rural landowners.

It is of interest to note that in the districts of Koraput, Kalahandi, Balangir and Sambhalpur, more quantum of land has been distributed than in coastal districts. The tribals or the rural poor could not take full advantage of the same because it was not followed by financial assistance for their cultivation which is a must at the initial stage of allotment otherwise the beneficiaries will be tempted to lease out their lands again, due to distress or inability to tide over the transitional vacuum of credit with them.

In Orissa, raiyati rights have been conferred on more that 1.6 lakh temporary lessees.

In the three tribal districts i.e. Kalahandi, Koraput and Phulbani, the incidence of tenancy seems to be low. The tribal tenants particularly Halas were treated as annual farm servants by landowners. The administrative machinery seems unconcerned about the gross violation of Fair Rent Provision in the statute. The NSS data reveal that 7.84% of the operated area was under tenancy during 1981-82. Orissa has prohibited future leases but in practice, it appears that informal tenancy persists. The informal tenants need to be conferred status of occupancy tenants and owners subsequently.

Tenancy Reforms

1. 'Share-croppers' should be recognized as 'tenants' in the state tenancy legislation.
2. The implementation of fair rent is tardy and ineffective. It should be vigorous and potent.

3. A special drive should be undertaken to unearth informal tenancy and implementation of Fair Rent.
4. 'Share-croppers' should be recorded first and then they should not be allowed to change the plots now and then.

Land Ceiling situation in Orissa

There is a need for a much closer scrutiny of the returns filed by landowners, specially the need to have a good second look at the question whether landowners who ought to have filed returns under the present land ceiling laws have really done so.

Lot of privileged raiyats are evading the dragnet of ceiling laws. They include cooperative societies, Lord Jagannath public trusts and public financial institutions. The poor cultivators, if allowed secured, permanent and heritable rights on such lands, will offer much more produce to Lord Jagannath as they are true devotees of Lord Jagannath.

For a family of five members a ceiling limit of five hectares for the best category of land with assured irrigation capable of raising at least two crops a year, 7.5 hec for the next category with assured irrigation for at least one crop a year and 12 hec. for all other lands is suggested.

The village record is the most crucial tool for ensuring efficient implementation of either ceiling or tenancy laws. Hence, its proper maintenance is essential.

Taking into account the observations on various loopholes in the existing law, it is clear that the best of the bureaucracy supported by flawless law, but unaided by the organizations of rural workers cannot achieve any significant success.

In a large part of Koraput district, the subtenants and under-raiyats were not recorded under the first settlements operations of 1962-63. In view of this, it is only to be expected that an important area of OLR Act has been inoperative in the District for all practical purposes.

The allottees belong to the landless category and they have got 0.8 hectares of land. The land allotted is of dry category and the productivity is very poor. The development assistance could be dovetailed to make the land more suitable for agriculture. But this has not happened. Moreover most of the tribal allottees have been doing podu-cultivation in the land allotted to them but that alone cannot sustain their livelihood.

In village Barafunds of district Kalahandi, the lands in some of the cases were not in the physical possession of the allottees and were under forcible occupation by farmers of the higher castes. In certain cases after the physical possession was given, the amount of land recorded was less than initially allotted.

However, there was no perceptible change in social and economic status of the allottees of land because of their poverty and extremely bad quality of the land distributed to them.

The financial inputs through banks and other financial institutions can help them to improve their conditions.

The land records in Orissa require thorough updating for which Central Government has placed lot of funds with the revenue department, Government of Orissa. Most of the funds are unutilized. This is high time that land records are updated. As a result lot of concealed land will surface and be available for distribution to a large number of dalits and adivasis in Orissa.

The opposition to land acquisition in Orissa also requires a thorough insight. If it is motivated by some vested interests led by a few NGOs, it should be overlooked by the Government. However, genuine demands of people should be taken care of by the popularly elected government.

16
Land Reforms in Andhra Pradesh

The State of Andhra Pradesh tops the list of Naxalite violence in the country. The figures are as follows;

Table 16.1: Naxalite Violence in Andhra Pradesh

Year	Incidents	Deaths
2003	577	140
2004	310	74
2005	335	208
2006	163	43

Table 16.2: Naxalite Violence in the Country

Year	Incidents	Deaths
2003	1597	515
2004	1533	566
2005	1608	677
2006	1272	610

Only during 2006–07, the new states of Chhattisgarh and Jharkhand are overtaking Andhra Pradesh.

Andhra Pradesh used to be one of the better organised states from land reforms point of view after independence. There is a good political party organization as well as a good revenue set-up. Therefore, we shall examine in details as to what has gone wrong.

A Comprehensive Law on the Ceiling on Agricultural Land Holdings was enacted and brought into force in Andhra Pradesh in 1975. At that time, it was estimated that over one million acres of distributable surplus land would be available. But it was noticed that the state government could take over only 0.54 million acres. What was more significant was that 0.258 million acres became embroiled in litigation at different stages. Every declarant who could afford it, moved the court. Often enough title verdicts favoured them. In the course of these ponderous litigations, several appeals which the Government decided to file could not be filed and where matters were carried to the Supreme Court, they found themselves in a queue of appeals and revisions which would take years to resolve.

In Andhra Pradesh "standard holding" range is from acres 10 to 27 wet and 35 to 54 dry. No scientific study has gone into the determination of a "standard holding" .

The State has enough problems to contend with in regard to agricultural land ceiling schemes. If the state government manages to bring the litigations to some conclusion pending in courts, substantial area will be available for distribution.

Another bane of the land reforms legislation has been the concealment of surplus land by the declarants. Unfortunately the Act does not provide for a "review" of the closed cases when any concealment is detected. Attempt has been made to correct this infirmity through legislative action. It is also proposed to provide for voluntary declaration by landowners if they had concealed any surplus land. Such declaration would save them from the punitive action provided in the Act.

Most tenancies in Andhra area are based on oral contracts. Barring a few cases, the land records are scarcely a guiding factor in determining as to who the tenant is. The Protected Tenancy Act was introduced in Telangana area in 1950. But six years previous to it, government ensured that the occupation of the lands by the tenants was properly recorded in the land records which eventually became the basis on which the tenants' rights and his legitimacy were established. For historical reasons, it was not so in Andhra area.

The state government having been fully conscious of the strong emotional attachment of the tribals to the landed properties, have accorded utmost importance to the problem of alienation of tribal lands in the scheduled areas. Special Regulations were made in exercise of the special legislative powers conferred under Fifth Schedule to the Constitution of India. The Regulations provide for the prevention of alienation of tribals land, and for restoration of the illegally alienated lands.

The A. P. Scheduled Areas Land Transfer Regulation 1959 which was amended in 1970, 1971 and 1978 is in force in the scheduled areas of the State. These Regulations were preceded by the local laws of the Madras province and Ex. Hyderabad State.

The Regulations prohibit several forms of transfer of land such as sale, lease, gift, mortgage, exchange etc. in favour of non-tribals. Whenever a transfer of land is made in the scheduled areas, it should be only in favour of a tribal or registered cooperative society consisting of only tribals. To support this measure, the Regulations also prohibit registration of transfer deeds unless the transfer is in favour of only a tribal or an exclusive tribal society.

A special machinery has been created to implement the Regulations effectively and to evict the non-tribals in illegal occupation of tribal lands and also to restore such lands to tribals. The Regulations also seek to pursue such non-tribals who acquire lands in contravention of the Regulations or who continue to remain in occupation of the lands even after they are evicted by the authorities with rigorous imprisonment for a period, up to one year. The Regulations of this State are unique in the country inasmuch as they prohibit transfer of not only tribals lands to non-tribals but also those of non- tribals unless they are transferred to tribals or their exclusive cooperative societies. This measure ensures prevention of the alienation of lands which the non-tribals illegally acquired from tribals in violation of the legal provisions. The Regulations do not affect the legitimate family partitions. Similarly, inheritance by succession is also not affected on account of the Regulations.

Recognising the position that the indebtedness of tribals is one of the important reasons contributing to the problem of land alienation, the government has brought out Debt Relief Regulations and Moneylending Regulations for redeeming the tribals from the indebtedness and to control and regulate private moneylending.

Besides, the state government has also recognised the need for the survey and updating of land records in the scheduled areas effectively combating the problem of tribal land alienation. Three special survey divisions with full complement of staff have been established for undertaking this task in parts of the scheduled areas where the problem is more acute.

In Andhra Pradesh, different provisions of land reforms are applicable to different regions. In Andhra area, the old Act of 1950 was repealed and a new Act, A.P. (Andhra Area) Tenancy Act 1956 was enacted. Similarly tenancy reform in Telangana is guided by the Tenancy and Agricultural Lands (Validation) Act 1961. The Telengana Act recognizes temporary leasing for six years which can be again renewed for the same period. A family holding in Telengana area varies between 4 and 60 acres.

The Andhra Pradesh Land Reforms Ceiling on Agricultural Holdings Act 1973 prescribes ceiling limit. The ceiling area of the family unit was fixed as equivalent to one standard holding with a maximum of two standard holding for a family unit in excess of five. In 1977 the Act was amended which allowed one additional standard holding for each major son. Nearly 4.45 lakh declarations were filed in the State but only 13.53% declarations were decided as surplus and remaining 86.4% were decided as non-surplus. The area declared as surplus is 5.25 lakh acres of which 93.76% was dry land and only 6.24% was wet land. Out of above, 3.8 lakh acres of land was assigned for agricultural purpose and 0.02 lakh acres were allotted for house sites. Thus, there was ineffectiveness of land ceiling programme in the State. Sometimes, provisions relating to 'personal cultivation' have been misused by the landlords to deprive the poor lessees or tenants-in-possession.

It is learnt that the State is trying to have a relook to rejuvenate land reforms set-up. At least, pending cases could be decided and possession to assignees of vested land would be given and updated land records will be handed over to each person.

Until 1966-67 rising in Srikakulam in Andhra Pradesh, the general belief was that rural India has always been a mass of sleeping villagers acquiescing in every form of injustice.

The Telengana Movement was aimed at restructuring agrarian social relations through direct action against the government. The government was thus, obliged to embark upon a radical land reform policy to wean the peasants away from militancy. The Telengana region has a high proportion of tenancy due to the prevalence of pervasive absentee landlordism.

The first round of land ceiling in AP in 1961 was an abysmal failure. Only about 7400 acres of land became available and very little land could actually be distributed to the poor against the estimated target of 30 lakh acres of land.

The second round of land ceilings legislation in 1973 was somewhat better. Against the estimated surplus of 20 lakh acres by 1992, about eight lakh acres were distributed, although much of this was dry land of inferior quality.

Problems

In Andhra Pradesh, the informal tenancy persists even in Telangana area where leasing is not permitted. The landless tenants are in a bad shape. The land taken on lease by them, keeps them at below subsistence level. The landowners frequently change their plots. They are mostly sharecroppers. They meet the entire cost of cultivation and receive less than 50 per cent share of produce.

The following anomalies still persist:

(i) The administrative machinery to identify and detect informal tenancy hardly exists.

(ii) The provision of conferring the status of occupancy tenants to sharecropper/ tenants-at-will is under neglect.

(iii) The right of continuous resumption without any time limit, provision of surrender, and loose definition of

'Personal Cultivation' continue to be the loopholes in the tenancy provisions of the State.

(iv) Lack of acquisition of optimum quantum of surplus land (3,64,168 out of 1,38,46,740 hectares).

(v) Distribution of poor quality of land partly government vested land. The average allotment from 1.4 to 1.7 acres, mostly dry land is insufficient to establish a self-sufficient holding, not to speak of any regular marketable surplus.

(vi) The domination of big farmers like politicians and merchants.

(vii) Exemption of cash plantation from ceiling laws.

Solutions

(i) The ceiling laws are very generous and they should be brought at par with other states as per the guidelines laid down by the Government of India.

(ii) Restriction of right of transfer of land in Telengana by the tenants for institutional credit is depriving the cultivators of land.

(iii) Training of Revenue officers.

(iv) Formation of new land tribunals.

(v) Functioning of Taluka level review committee relating to land reforms.

(vi) Updating of land records in the State.

(vii) Disposal of returns/cases relating to ceiling surplus land should be done on the basis of operation mode.

(viii) Ensuring institutional credit to the assignees of government vested land.

(ix) The greatest drawback of the Act is that it does not envisage suo-moto taking up of cases. The special officer can at best play the role of an adjudicator when moved and cannot take up cases himself for protection of even registered tenants.

(x) The definition of 'Personal Cultivation' is vague.

(xi) The Tenancy Act should recognize oral agreements,

(xii) The burden of proof should rest on the landowner not only in the context of fixation of fair rent but also in respect of all other matters like 'Personal Cultivation'.

(xiii) Tenancy reform can be implemented only through revenue department and all disputes relating to such matters should be adjudicated by competent revenue official. The jurisdiction of the judicial official should be restricted.

(xiv) The right of resumption seriously affects security of tenure. It should be abolished.

(xv) The rent is still on the high side. It should be fixed at 1/5 of gross produce.

The glaring ineffectiveness of land ceiling measures is borne out from the fact that only 13.53 per cent declarations were decided as surplus and remaining 86.47 per cent were decided as non-surplus. The area declared as surplus is 5.25 lakh acres of which 93.76 per cent was dry land and only 6.24 per cent was wet land. In several cases, assignment has been done on papers. Physical possession has not been handed over to the assignees. Further, the assigned lands have not been demarcated on ground levels in many cases. In spite of irrigation potentialities created over course of time, the land records continue to show it as dry land.

"The ineffectiveness of land ceiling programme in the State tends to be further corroborated from the following facts. The empirical study in the villages shows that 30 per cent of the area allotted was completely uncultivable and 67 per cent of the allotted land was unirrigated. The average extent of land allotted was not economically viable. This suggests that land ceiling programme in Andhra Pradesh was a failure. Besides this, of the total extent of land distributed in the surveyed villages only 6.91 per cent was allotted to scheduled castes and 32.79 per cent was allotted to schedule tribes. The State ceiling rules prescribed that at least half of the declared surplus land should be allotted to scheduled castes and scheduled tribes. In surveyed villages the allotment of land to these two categories falls short by at least 10.40 per cent of the prescribed requirement. The distribution of land is further titled against scheduled tribes in particular. The uncultivable land, in one of the villages, to the extent of 54.55 hec. was allotted to 30 scheduled tribes which amounted to 1.82 hec. per scheduled tribe beneficiary.[1]

The cumulative problem of implementation of land ceiling laws for the quarter ending December, 2007 is as follows;

(Area in acres)

Returns			Area declared surplus	Area taken possession	Area distributed to individual beneficiaries	Total No. of beneficiaries	SC/ST beneficiaries			
Filed	Disposed	Pending					SC Beneficiaries		ST Beneficiaries	
							No	Area	No	Area
447103	417279	29824	837840	653944	593944	532078	205126	229656	85758	120277

Other Beneficiaries		Area Declared Surplus but not distributed	Total No. of Cases and Area involved in Litigation		Revenue Courts		High Courts		Supreme Court	
No.	Area	Area	Area Involved	No. of Cases	Area	No.	Area	No.	Area	No.
195019	243933	243896	131570	2193	86694	1111	35933	874	8943	208

Area not available for distribution			Total Area not available for distribution	Net Area available for distribution
Reserved/ Transferred for public purpose	Unifit for cultivation	Misc. reasons		
16717	13673	14859	176819	67077

In Andhra 43.93 lakh areas of wasteland and 1.10 lakh acres of Bhoodan land out of total 2.52 lakh acres of Bhoodan land have been distributed. There is lot of scope for distribution of 1.42 lakh acres of Bhoodan land, lot of wasteland and 80,000 acres of land available under the ceiling laws. Equally, there is scope for further vesting of surplus land to Government because 29,824 returns are still pending for disposal. As per an estimate

---

1 Iyer, Prof. K. Gopal : *Report on Empirical Study on Land Reforms in India*, page 97, published by LBS National Academy of Administration, Mussourie.

and as per statement in the Assembly during the AP Land Reforms (Ceiling on Agricultural Holdings) Act 1973, about 20 lakh acres of land would be surplus whereas at present only 8,37,840 acres of land could be declared surplus indicating an achievement of 40 per cent. Out of the surplus land, 2,43,896 acres land is yet to be distributed. This includes 1,31,570 acres of land which is involved in litigation. Revenue courts above account for pendency of 86,694 acres of land. The Govt. of Andhra Pradesh or department of revenue rather than blaming the High Courts or Supreme Court, should introspect and gear up its quasi-judicial machinery of revenue courts and fix up their responsibility for non-disposal of cases or delay in disposal of cases. However, most of the land determined as surplus is dug, which under the given climate condition implies low and insecure yields. Thus, the average land allotted to each beneficiary is too small to offer full employment or livelihood for a family of four or five persons. Most of the distributed land is in need of civilisation, levelling and other developmental activities. The Central Government has planned to assist these new small land holders either by special schemes or by integration into existing schemes. George and Rao (1979) have made a pilot study in two villages in Nalgonda district. According to them, the new cultivators, who are beneficiaries of the reform, have invested in their land and developed it, though the quality is poor. They have borne all costs, earned a surplus and built up their assets. Thus, the new land reform beneficiaries are a solid base for increase in production because they cultivate their holdings with a higher intensity of labour per hectare. "However, there is altogether different story regarding allocation of the government wasteland. "Field investigations in Andhra Pradesh for example, indicate that perhaps as much as 30 per cent of the reported beneficiaries do not have both legal and physical possession of the allocated land. The gaps between the reported numbers and secure land rights occur for a variety of reasons, including;

i) assignment of land is on paper only, and the beneficiaries are not in physical possession;

ii) more powerful have enacted the beneficiaries from their land and;

iii) in numerous cases, especially in Telengana where large compact blocks have been assigned to the poor, the beneficiaries have not received their individual parcels of land because the survey sub-division work is incomplete"[2]

Andhra Pradesh's recent efforts to address the 'gaps' in allocation of govt. land provide a model for other states to consider. Andhra Pradesh's IKP project identifies often with the help of the community-based organisations—specific local opportunities or developmental schemes or assistance for enhancing the poor's rights to government land. The joint efforts of the revenue department, IKP and numerous state officials and local communities or panchayat bodies have put secure rights to at least lakh of acres of government into the lands of the rural people. Government of Andhra Pradesh recognised the good work done by the CPI(Maoist) in October 2004 when they agreed to a case file and promised to consider in the meantime the Naxalites main demand for distribution of land among the landless. The state government also agreed to consider the landless or poor cultivations for allotment of government surplus land who were put in forcible possession by the Naxalites. There should be no opposition to it. Even in West Bengal, the first priority in land allotment goes to the person in possession provided he is otherwise eligible. This is just to keep peace in rural India because ownership is 9/10th of possession. In West Bengal, the CPI(M) and other parties identify the excess land of the ex-Zamindars, jotder or the landowners through their own technical wing and then put its landless people or marginal farmers into the possession of surplus land lying either uncultivated, or in benami names or is in excess of ceiling limit. Then, the priority lists are made at the block level or panchayat samity in consultation with the local pradhan and then get resolution passed to distribute these surplus land among the eligible beneficiaries. If Naxalites adopt the same technique or procedure, what hell can fall upon the government machinery. They are just assisting the government machinery to make preliminary lists of the eligible beneficiaries. One should not be opposed to a sound proposal/offer, if it has come from the Naxalite camps. 'opposition for opposition' sake is counterproductive.

---

[2] Tom Hamstad, T. Haque, Robin Nelson : *Improving Land Access for India's Rural,* Page 54, *EPW*, March 8, 2008

Tenancy Reform

Total number of tenants recorded in Andhra Pradesh as in December are 1.07 lakh on an area of 5.95 lakh acres. The latest research studies[3] indicate that the informal/concealed tenancy in the coastal Andhra ranges from 15 to 30 per cent of the total owned area.

Thus, oral tenancy requires to be recognized in AP and the period of lease in case of sharecroppers should be extended at least during his lifetime and no longer.

Tribal Land

Andhra Pradesh has a very long record of legislation for the protection of tribal land. There are large tracts of tribal land which are still under the occupation of the non-tribals. For example, as in March 2004, the status on alienation and restoration of Tribal Lands in Andhra Pradesh is as follows:

1 No. of cases filed in the Courts: 65875

2 Area: 287776 (acres)

3 Cases disposed of by the Courts: 58212

4 Area: 256452 (acres)

5 Cases rejected: 31737

6 Area involved: 150227 (acres)

7 Cases decided in favour of tribals: 26475

8 Area: 106225 (acres)

9 Cases in which land was restored to tribals: 23383

10 Area: 94312 (acre)

(Source: Annual Report, 2004-2005, Ministry of Rural Development, Government of India, page 213).

Thus, only one-third of the total area alienated has been restored to them. Besides, they are subjected to displacement from thousands of acres due to various development projects and

---

3 Bergmann, Theodor: *Agrarian Reform,* p126, published by Agricole Publishing Academy, New Delhi.

evictions by forest department on the plea of encroachment of forestland. The Samta Judgement and the Panchayat Extension Act of 1996 are silver linings in this respect which should be utilized by the present organizations in protecting the land rights of the tribals[4].

Updating of Land Records—A New Approach

Andhra Pradesh is spearheading campaign to update land records along with Karnataka and West Bengal. The Government of Andhra Pradesh have taken up a novel project called Bhu Bharati with an object to establish a comprehensive system of land administration based on secured titles and title registration, leveraging the available technology. This project also involves legal reforms, process re-engineering and administrative restructuring. Andhra Pradesh has drafted a Bill titled the Andhra Pradesh Land Titling Act, 2008.

The statement of Objects and Reasons of the above Act reads as follows;

"In India, records relating to immovable property transactions are dealt with in the form of documents and such documents are got registered under the Registration Act 1908. In the document registration system, title verification is not done. With India's rapid movement into the technological age, there is every need to ensure maximum utilization of Land as a resource, by introducing title registration system, which gives scope for growth in Land market with reduced litigation in courts.

In order to improve the system of land administration, and to ensure, security of titles to the property holders, the state of Andhra Pradesh seeks to enact a novel legislation for putting in place a mechanism for a Land Information System and an Authority to manage the same, with the following broad objectives:

- To provide for creation and maintenance of a record of all immovable properties in the state of Andhra Pradesh, so as to serve as conclusive record of titles

4. Iyer, K. Gopal : Paper on *'Land Reforms and State Repression"*, presented in the Hyderabad convention titled 'Status of Land Reforms in A.P. and the need to implement Radical Land Reforms'.

- To provide for title registration system
- To provide for a mechanism for ensuring that land records data in the state of Andhra Pradesh is captured and maintained in digital form and in an integrated manner.
- To ensure that the information pertaining to the records maintained by the Andhra Pradesh Land Authority is protected from any unauthorized access and provide for the establishment of the efficient security system for such purpose.
- To provide for a special adjudicatory authority for the efficient and speedy resolution of disputes arising out of the operation of this legislation."

This is a good invitation undertaken by the Directorate of Survey, Settlements and Land Records. This is possible in Andhra Pradesh because there is already an infrastructure of Common Service Centre(CSC) existing throughout the state where all services converge and are available to citizens. Andhra Pradesh is the first State perhaps in the country which could integrate registration with change of land records through process of mutation and conversion. In other states, it will take long time due to interdepartmental quibbling as registration and maintenance of land records are with two different departments. As soon as, it is done, better it is. The Central Government has given such a guideline. But states take their own time to implement even the best of policies enunciated by the Central Government.

The suggestions to improve upon the maintenance of proposed land records and titling system are as follows;

1. Registration should be linked with the incorporation of the same in the record-of-rights. Record-of-rights may be prepared according to the possession or rather verification of each and every plot of the concerned 'mouza' supported by a deed of transfer or inheritance or partition or exchange etc.
2. Together with the titling in the record-of-rights, there should be a noting in the possession column of the record-of-rights in order to the alteration in the mode of cultivation, for example, by a bargadar/share-cropper.

3. The Land Titling Appellate Tribunal should be above Land Authority and this Tribunal may consist of a chairman who will be a sitting or retired judge of High Court and other judicial members along with senior administrative members conversant with the various land laws of the State. The persons aggrieved by the judgement of such Tribunal may prefer an appeal to the Division Bench of High Court formed for the purpose.

4. There should be a family ceiling for determination of ceiling area in case of every raiyat. Persons aggrieved by the decision should go to the newly proposed land Titling Appellate Tribunal.

5. The excess land so determined may be distributed to the landless/homeless people in the area concerned. The Panchayat functionaries along with the revenue officials who are conversant with the geographical position and socio-economic condition of the concerned mouza/ village should be delivered the power to determine as to who would be selected to be issued patta in his/ her favour. Joint pattas may be issued in the names of husband and wife.

6. Special provisions should be made for incorporation of the names of the bargadars and pattadars as suggested above.

7. A Corporation in order to advance funds to a recorded bargadar or a landless person may be formed for the benefit of the landless people and bargadars belonging to the low rung of the society. If any such person intends to sell out land, such corporation may provide finance to such person for purchase of such land according to the assessed marked value of the land to be sold for the purpose. In this case Sec. 21(c) of the West Bengal Land Reforms Act 1955 may be consulted.

8. The Government of Andhra Pradesh may like to place the fact of digitized maps in the Act and digitized map along with the records-of-right will be given to the individual raiyat as record-of-rights which will have proper boundaries

of the plot with the adjoining plots. Thus this type record-of-right will be the best record of right in the country. It should be mandatory that after 10 years there should be compulsory updating of record-of-rights by the State.

9. The Bargadars and Pattadars may be given financial support annually in the form of credit or subsidy by the bank and by the State Govt. for cultivation of crop. This may find place in the proposed Act.

10. In case the Government does not find suitable government surplus land for allotment to the landless persons, the Govt. may purchase the land from the willing persons on the market value and may allot the land to the landless person up to 16 decimal of land so that this small piece of land may support him for his livelihood and will save him from starvation. This may be done on the pattern of similar scheme in West Bengal.

Conclusion

1. Remaining banjar land in tribal areas should be surveyed on time bound fashion and should be distributed among the tribals.

2. Land ceiling exemptions for temple lands, charitable trusts, plantations should be withdrawn unless they agree to come directly under the Government.

3. "Absentee landlordism' specially in coastal Andhra and Telengana Region should be discouraged and definition of personal cultivation should be incorporated in the A.P. Act on the pattern of definition of 'personal cultivation' in Section 2(8) of the W.B. Land Reforms Act 1956, which reads as follows; "Personal Cultivation" means cultivation by a person of his own land or his own account –

   a) by his own labour, or

   b) by the labour of any member of his family, or

   c) by servants or labourers on wages payable in cash or kind not being as a share of the produce or both; provided that such person or member of his family resides for the greater part of the year in the locality where the land is situated and the principal source of his income is produce of such land.

4. Encroachments from government lands should be removed and surplus lands should be distributed among the landlords or poor cultivators.
5. Priority should be given in distribution of government vested land to those eligible persons who are already in possession of land and are cultivating the same.
6. Exemption for 'brackish water' and 'aclqua farms' should be withdrawn and retrieved land should be distributed to among agricultural labourers and fishermen unless they make cooperative society of these workers and earmark their land as owner in that society.
7. The tribal lands illegally transferred should be restored to the tribals.
8. Informal sharecropping or tenancy should be recorded only upto the life time of the sharecropper, unlike in West Bengal which is heritable. Thus 15 per cent to 30 per cent of total owned lands can be recorded under tenancy without ownership only for right of cultivation by the tenant.

If some of these suggestions are implemented in time spirit in a time bound fashion, Andhra Pradesh will soon come out of menace of Naxalism.

17

Components of Land Reforms in Karnataka

The institutional financing and political will are essential components of land reforms. Karnataka which is a proud Information Technology giant State in India, is the latest victim of Naxalism. During 2005, there were eight Naxalite incidents causing eight deaths and the trend is continuing. Let us examine where Karnataka has not done well and which is causing concern to the rural landless poor or the sharecroppers.

Deficiencies in Distribution of Land in Karnataka

The eligibility for the grant of land for agricultural purpose is:

a) the person must have attained the age of 18;

b) his gross annual income should not exceed Rs.4,800 as per Amendment Act., 2003

c) he should either be a bonafide agriculturist cultivating land personally or have a bonafide intention of utilizing land for personal cultivation and;

d) he should not be a sufficient landholder.

However, in case of the ex-servicemen and soldier, land may be granted if the gross annual income of the applicant does not exceed Rs.12,000/-.

The extent of land granted to any person should not exceed the prescribed limit, including land already held by him.

However, following reservation of land for distribution leaves no discretion with the local authority or panchayat body to deviate in deserving cases.

a) ex-servicemen and soldiers - 10 per cent

b) person belonging to the SCs & STs - 50 per cent

c) backward tribes - 05 per cent

d) political sufferers - 10 per cent

e) others - 25 per cent

The salutary principal in land distribution is that the land should be given to the one who cultivates the land personally so that production increases. Land is not donation or gift. It is for landless people who are capable enough physically to cultivate land and have been habitually, traditionally or practically doing the job of cultivation. Allotment of land to ex-servicemen and political sufferers is now out of context. The priority list for distribution of land should be ideally laid down as follows like in West Bengal.

i) First priority — Landless Scheduled Tribe

ii) Second priority — Landless Scheduled Caste

iii) The ceiling for allotment of land should be one acre. Persons who already hold less than one acre of land may, however be given land to an extent which is equal to the difference between one acre and the land already held by them.

iv) In case of a sharecropper or tenant, half of the land cultivated by him as a sharecropper is taken into account in computing this total land upto one acre.

v) The Sthayee Samiti or sub committee on land of the Panchayat Samiti at the block or taluka level may advise local revenue official in the matter of allotment.

vi) No settlement of land is to be made with a person who is employed in a business trade, undertaking service or industrial occupation etc.

Thus, general cultivators will come under consideration after BPL category STs and SCs are considered first for allotment of land. These BPL category list of persons is ready made available at each panchayat level and can be used to draw up priority list for allotment. First preference is to be given to the person in possession of land but only upto one acre of land. In that case, he will get priority even over and above scheduled tribe and scheduled caste cultivators or agricultural labourers or the landless persons as because disturbance in possession may lead to a war between the two poor persons which is not the aim of the land reform measures.

However, limit for allotment for home-stead should be 0.0339 ha which comes to about eight decimal and is sufficient for a house alongwith cattle and kitchen garden. The deed of settlement known as patta is issued in the name of the Governor and the land is not transferable but is heritable. The name of wife is also written jointly in West Bengal in view of gender justice. Possession is given simultaneously because land without possession has no meaning.

As the allotment of land and delivery of possession cut links of the allottee with the landowner who is also his money lender, the financial institution like banks, cooperative societies or service-cooperatives should immediately step in otherwise he will again mortgage the land to the erstwhile landowner.

A survey by IAS probationers of the LBS National Academy of Administration brings out the following fallacies in land distribution in Karnataka,

a) The norms of allotment in about half of the quantum of land allotted have been violated.

b) The package of economic assistance alongwith land allotment was lacking.

c) The encroachment of land mainly in Bangalore district has been done by the powerful and ineligible persons.

Thus, this is high time that injustice done to the underprivileged persons should be undone and they should he given government surplus land.

They should, in a big way, be assisted for crop finance loan on concessional rate of interest and government subsidy or schemes to reclaim and develop their barren or waste land through various water harvesting schemes.

It is surprising to note that as in December 2007 about 1,15,765 acres of land was not distributed out of a total area of 2,41,710 acres of land which is the poorest performance among all States (as per GOI report). Even before taking over possession, lot of land got involved in litigation. This shows utter callousness. The vesting of land and taking over possession are simultaneous processes. At least paper possession is taken by the government which is also provided generally in most of the land reforms legislations. One fails to understand what State government of Karnataka has been doing with 45,343 acres of land pending in 1,505 cases at the High Court which is the highest in the country. Even in revenue courts 15,682 acres of land is locked. Karnataka is the first State to set up the Land Tribunal which should be an alternative to the High Court. One fails to understand why the cases from High Court were not transferred to the Karnataka Land Tribunal. It is not understood why 38,008 acres of land is not being distributed which is held up for miscellaneous reasons. Failure of the State government in this most important field of land reform gives ample reason why the Naxalism is raising its head in otherwise peace loving, proadministration and prosperous State of Karnataka.

Karnataka has done well in promoting distribution of homestead plots as per study conducted by the Rural Development Institute, New York, USA. These homestead plots upto 15/16 decimal have been successfully used for vegetable and fruit cultivation and partly evergreen cultivation. These plots at least save the beneficiaries from starvation and put stability in their minds. This scheme is known as Ashraya scheme and even panchayats are purchasing land from free markets and are distributing among the deserving landless persons successfully. The homestead – cum – garden plot of at least 2178 sq. feet and up to 6544 sq.feet deserve serious consideration and these are to be dovetailed with the Indira Avas Yojna of the ministry of rural development, Government of India.

Karnataka has also done well by distributing 13.72 lakh acres of government waste land which requires to be developed further through various government schemes on liberal financial grants or loans.

Tenancy Reforms

Karnataka is in line with at least seven other States in India which have banned land tenancy. After conferment of ownership on about six lakh tenants, the State is resting on its laurels that it has done whatever was required for the tenant or the sharecroppers. But, in fact, informal tenancy exists all over the State. The tenancy that persists in the field is concealed/oral and the names of tenants are not entered in the revenue records. In 1981–82, 6.04 per cent of the operated area was leased-in in the State despite legal abolition of tenancy. The average area leased-in by the tenant was 4.76 acre.

The study by IAS probationers shows that of all tenants, 62.5 per cent have leased-in on sharecropping terms, 22.9 per cent on fixed cash rent terms, and 14.6 per cent on fixed rent terms in kind. Similarly, of the total area leased-in 59.6 per cent is under sharecropping, 21.6 per cent under fixed rent terms in kind, and 18.8 per cent under fixed cash rent terms. The profile of the tenants reveals the following :

a) Most of the pure tenants live below subsistence level.

b) The proportions of tenants living at above subsistence level are much higher among the owner-cum-tenants, some of whom fall in the category of rich peasants.

c) In view of low economic status of tenants, and also because most of them are concealed tenants, the question of tenancy reforms is an important one for all of them except those in the rich peasant category.

d) The tenants/owners are drawn from all the castes.

In a survey of agriculturists in Karnataka in 2000, the Rural Development Institute, Bangalore found:

1. 45 per cent of the respondents answering definitively state that tenancy prohibitions should be lifted;

2. 94 per cent of respondents answering definitively state that existing tenancy restrictions harm the landless;
3. 38 per cent respondents answering definitively report that at least one farmer in their village keeps land fallow rather than renting it out because renting may lead to the loss of such land.

Benefits of Relaxation

There is a need for changing the existing tenancy prohibition policy in Karnataka into one regulating it instead of banning it. Such regulating law will have, as revealed in other states, more beneficial effects, the significant ones being :

1. Removal of tenancy ban makes more lands available for landless poor to cultivate, at least as tenants;
2. Relaxation of prohibition allows lease of land for more productive use, diversification of agriculture and contract farming;
3. Tenancy regulation provides tenure security to cultivators and regulates rentals and brings in transparency;
4. Tenure security enables tenants to borrow credit, obtain input subsidies and other extension services easily;
5. Tenancy relaxation eliminates land left fallow for fear of losing it;
6. Permission to lease out eliminates unavoidable social conflict, insecurity of losing land as collateral security and social status symbol;
7. Equity issues can be addressed by reasonably fixing rental levels and providing tenure security to cultivators;
8. Ceiling limits on total holdings both for tenants and owners or partly as one and partly as other may be regulated to ensure equitable distribution of land which will meet demands of equity;
9. Tenancy regulation along with reasonable ceiling limit would render farming economically viable; and

10. Having achieved removal of exploitative intermediaries, zamindar, jagirdars and inamdars, tenancy prohibition is no longer necessary. On the other hand, there is need to regulate commercial type of leases by companies to prevent "new baniyas" converting farmers into "new serfs".

The informal tenants or sharecroppers on the basis of 'barga operation' of West Bengal can be recorded as follows :

i) Composite squads of the land revenue machinery and settlement department should be made by revenue officer or kanungo.

ii) The squad will work in specified pockets where concentration of tenants as per report of panchayats and district land reforms officer or settlement officer is more.

iii) The panchayat or members of local political party will collect applications in bulk.

iv) Then the squad should go and hold evening meeting in a mauza or group of villages where the recording of sharecroppers will take place and explain the procedure so that the tenants and landowners may attend recording process without fear or favour.

v) After hearing both sides, parcha or record of recording will be handed over to the sharecropper alongwith the details of plots, he cultivates in an impartial and objective manner.

vi) These squads will be legally empowered by the Government through suitable notification or notifications.

Contract Farming

In Karnataka, the contract farming has some good dividends specially in the field of exports of coffee, spices, fresh fruits, flower, cashew, vegetables, gherkins and raisins.

Some of the even marginalized farmers have made tons of money by adopting above types of crops and selling them through the corporates or agri-export zones. Gherkins alone has got

Rs. 140 to 150 crore export markets every year. Rose, Onions were exported from the state during 2005-06 for Rs. 50 crore. The total area covered and the farmers involved in contract farming in Karnataka is still less then one per cent. In the meantime, the corporates have started seeking to lease out their lands which should not be permitted creating new brand of zamindars and landlords. The experiment is to be kept under watch for some more years. If the benefits reach directly to the farmers in a substantial quantum, than the contract farming can be further promoted by relaxation of ceiling laws and tenancy laws on those farmers. It is still demanded from the corporate that they may involve farmers whose lands they have acquired not as daily labourers but as shareholders or individual owners in the form of cooperative farming or the registered society etc. If Naxalism spreads due to contract farming, then the contract farming will have to be discontinued.

Updation of Land Records

Karnataka is the leader in the field and has been awarded by Government of India in this regard. Karnataka has good revenue set-up and the machinery is quite motivated. It is estimated that all records-of-rights alongwith maps of plots of individual raiyats or owners have been computerized in Karnataka and people can have most updated records-of-rights. Thus, it is clear that Karnataka can venture successfully to bring about all types of land reforms to tackle the problem of Naxalism in the State.

Suggestions

1. The balance ceiling surplus and government waste land should be distributed without further delay giving top priority to the scheduled tribes specially in the Naxalites affected areas/talukas of the State.
2. The priority list for the land reform beneficiaries needs suitable amendment. Land is for those who cultivate land personally.
3. The existing tenancy prohibition policy should be changed into tenancy regulation policy.

4. Informed tenants or sharecroppers should be recorded in Karnataka on the pattern of 'barga operation' in West Bengal and involvement of the Land Tribunal should be only as the final appellate tribunal.
5. The scheme for distribution of homestead cum kitchen garden plots requires further encouragement and patronage by government and panchayats.
6. Extensive schemes should be implemented for reclaiming and developing government land also by dovetailing various rural development schemes.
7. Efforts should be made to link up transfer of lands through registration with updation of land records through normal processes of mutation and conversion. Karnataka should attempt to give map of plots along with the records-of-rights or copy of khatian with respect to village boundary and adjoining plot configuration as is being experimented in West Bengal. This will combine best points of both rayatwari system in south and permanent settlement system in rest of the country.

It is hoped that the good network of revenue and settlement administration will soon tide over temporary show of discontent in the form of Naxalism. The resurgent revenue administration led by requisite 'political will' will be able to contain Naxalism in the State.

18

Land Reforms in Maharashtra

The implementation of land reforms in Maharashtra is beset by bottlenecks. The execution of agrarian reform laws was periodically reviewed by the State government and the first such comprehensive review was undertaken as far back as in 1972. The only intermediary tenures that are being continued today are the Devasthan and Wakf Inam grants.

Abolition of the intermediaries resulted in the conferment of occupancy rights on a very large body of under-right holders and some tenants in all parts of the State. This could indeed be said to be the first major step towards the transition of a feudal order to democratic social order.

The Maharashtra Agricultural Lands (Ceiling on Holdings) Act, 1961 came into force on 26th January 1962. An area measuring 1,24,493 ha. was declared surplus under the provisions of the said Act.

The ceiling were lowered in 1975, as a consequence of which an area of 1,60,962 ha. was declared as surplus. Out of the total area of 2,85,455 ha, 2,51,522 ha. have already been distributed.

Land measuring 18,422 ha. had to be excluded from distribution because this was either uncultivable or needed for public purposes or was involved in exemption claims. An area of 6,204 hectares is involved in litigation.

The proportion of scheduled castes and scheduled tribes allottees in Maharashtra has been as high as 53%. The ceiling which was initially imposed on agricultural holdings in 1962, was substantially lowered within a short span of just about 13 years.

The very fact that the lands declared surplus under the Amended Act of 1975 were considerably more than what had been acquired under the Principal Act, is proof enough of the fact that the Act was implemented quite successfully in Maharashtra. Maharashtra's performance as far as implementation of the Ceiling Act is concerned, therefore, speaks for itself. These ceilings will be further lowered with the passage of time by the operation of the laws of succession.

Tribal Land Alienation

The law relating to the prevention of alienation of tribal holdings in favour of non-tribals is sufficiently stringent in Maharashtra. Government has also taken steps to ensure restoration of land which had been transferred by the tribals in favour of non-tribals under due process of law, to the tribals. Lands measuring 43,351 ha. have been restored to the tribals under these measures. Immediate concern is to augment the compensation admissible to the non-tribals.

Though a redistribution of the ceiling surplus land has gone a long way in the expansion of the owner cultivation came by a "politically costless" means unavailable to other crowded states like Kerala and West Bengal. This was the distribution of just over a million acres of cultivable wasteland.

However, it will be wrong to presume that the political leaders in Maharashtra had any intention or the political will to implement the land reform legislation seriously and honestly. It is a well known fact that in Maharashtra the dominant political class comes from the rich peasantry. The rich sugar barons control the political leadership of the State. Even the then Chief known for his concern for land reforms, had spoken publicly of the economic, political and the administrative arguments for retaining the old ceiling limits in 1971. At the time, even the lower rank of hegemonic Congress Party in Maharashtra came in open revolt against the new ceiling law, to be promulgated and implemented. As a result, the Ceiling Act of 1975 (implemented in 1978) did not change the ceiling limit at 18 acres for the most valuable land (irrigated land).

As the revenue department has become a general administration department, it has utterly neglected its original revenue work. The records were not updated. In backward and hilly districts, where Naxalites are active, neither the landowners nor revenue officers cared to record the changes in revenue records. As a result, the landlords as well as small and marginal farmers were harassed by the talathis who are custodian of record-of-rights.

If records-of-rights are not up to date, further lands can not be vested to the State nor benami lands can be unearthed. The poor people who were given patta or government land were not recorded in revenue records. They thus, were at the mercy of revenue officials (talathis) or the earstwhile landlords who continued to occupy their entire lands though it got vested to State by law.

Tenancy Reforms

The Tenancy legislations are different for the three regions of Maharashtra. The Mumbai Region is covered by the Bombay Tenancy and Agriculture Land Act 1948 and (Amendment) Act 1955; the Marathwada region is guided by the Hyderabad Tenancy and Agriculture Land Act 1950, the Bombay Tenancy and Agricultural Act 1958 (Vidarbha Region and Kutch Area) applies to the rest. The provisions of each are similar. They provide for fixity of rent, security of tenure and compulsory transfer of land to the tenants which are non-resumable by landlords.

State of Maharashtra gives two extreme situations. Towards Vidarbha region, the share-coppers or the landless persons feel deprived of their rights whereas the tenant in Pune, Kolhapur belt is sometimes richer than the landowner himself. Most of them have been working with their landowners for more than 10 years. The tenants after the 'Tillers Day' were entitled to purchase the tenancy within one year. The Government run co-operative farm under Maharashtra State Farming Development Corporation in Pune demonstrates an ideal system where the individual farmer can retain the ownership and can cultivate collectively. The cause of disparities in various regions in Maharashtra requires a close look. The experiment has been done in Maharashtra itself.

The problem is to undertake the implementation of this successful experiment to all parts of State without caring for political backlash. Then, only the extremists movement which is raising head here and there, can be tackled effectively and its further spread can be checked engulfing other regions of Maharashtra which happens to be one of the richest and most forward looking States of India.

Suggestions

1. After the 'Tillers Day' no attempt has been made so far to enrol the new informal tenants. A special drive should be undertaken to identify informal tenants and confer ownership rights on them.
2. The definition of 'Tenancy' should be broadened so as to include cash rent/kind rent and cropshares.
3. No surrender of tenancy should be permitted as these surrenders are generally forged or are managed in an emergency situation to a tenant or share-cropper.
4. In Vidarbha Region, the resumption of land by the landowners for personal cultivation up to three family holdings (i.e. from 21 to 120 acres) should be reduced. The definition of 'Personal Cultivation' should not include cultivation by hired labour under one's personal supervision.
5. Tenants conferred with ownership rights have to be directly integrated with the anti-poverty programmes.

In Maharashtra, by 1970, ownership of leased land was partly or fully transferred to the tenants in about 18.75 lakh tenancy cases out of a total of about 26 lakh recorded tenancy cases in the State.

In Maharashtra it is found that the incidence of tenancy is very low which was found on survey by the IAS probationers to the tune of 2.4 per cent. As per the NSS (National Sample Survey), 26th and 37th Round in 1971–72 it was 6.15 per cent and in 1981–82 it was 5.20 per cent. This is poorer than other states. Efforts should be made for recording of tenants. There is a phenomenon of 'reverse tenancy' where some small landholders holding land below two ha. lease out their land to relatively big holders who made good output of sugarcane by merging leased-in land with their own land. However, State of Maharashtra have done quite a good job by giving finance to the land allottees.

In fact, many tenants were neither aware of the provision of the Tiller's Day nor they were allowed to exercise this right of purchase. The landlords were obviously not only reluctant, but even opposed the acceptance of the tenancies as they feared that they would lose to these lands permanently and the tenants would become owners of their lands. The phenomenon prevailed all over Maharashtra, but especially in the four districts of the Konkan region where it was quite rampant. In Konkan districts, the informed tenants got organised to record their tenancy rights, similarly in Vidarbha region and Marathwada regions, they joined Naxalite outfits as they virtually got no support either from the ruling party or from the revenue administration for preserving their right of cultivation which is very basic to the rural poor.

Following weaknesses for bottlenecks were further noticed in implementation of land reform measures.

1) Absence of correct and updated records and lack of knowledge on the part of sharecroppers to know the details of lands, they cultivate.

2) Lack of financial support for land reform programmes. As a result, they take refuge of the local moneylenders who exploit them fully.

3) Weakness and irregularity of the reporting system and of evaluation.

4) Delay in disposal of cases by revenue courts as well as civil courts and the High Court.

In Maharashtra, Sawant (1991) estimated that about 44.6% of the total tenancy area was under concealed tenancy during 1981-82. Second, the type of exemptions allowed included exclusion of a landlord who was a minor, widow, serving in the armed forces or mentally and physically disabled. In addition to these, exemption was also given to a landlord who preferred to retain the land for self-cultivation in case the landlord did not have any other means of livelihood. Third, the clause of voluntary surrender by the tenant of his claim on the land had also rendered the legislation ineffective in many cases.

As in September 2006, 14.92 lakh tenants were conferred ownership rights on 42.90 lakh acres of land which is a better figure than West Bengal.

Distribution of land

Maharashtra has also been doing a good work in the field of distribution of government wasteland. Total of about 10.22 lakh acres Government wastelands have been distributed in Maharashtra and the process is still continuing since April, 2007 to February 2008, Maharashtra is leading in distribution of government wasteland which is 1,72,059 ha.

However, Maharashtra is lagging behind in the distribution of Bhoodan land though it is the native land of Vinoba. Maharashtra has still to distribute 77,000 acres of Bhoodan land. Similarly, Maharashtra doesn't maintain proper account of land vested to government and distributed. The total percentage of land distributed is 97.15% as per an estimate in December, 1995. However, there is a lot of gap in taking over possession of lands because lands get involved in court cases and this delays their take over. This is an area the State should pursue with all its might.

Some major implementation problems of the ceiling are :

1) The definition of the family unit, which included minor children, caused a serious problem. The limit of members to enjoy family ceiling should be restricted to five. Then, some additional area can be allowed. For less number of members in family, proportionate land for family should be deducted.
2) The partition of land was undertaken immediately so as to create separate family units.
3) The emergence of benami transactions was huge. The enquiry should be done in case of non-existing persons and should be disallowed.

4) The law provides that if a portion of land was leased out to a tenant, then such land should be excluded for the total size of holding of the family. This provision should not be there. Taking clue for this, a number of landholders created temporary false tenancy records in the names of permanent servants and avoided land transfer.

5) The categorisation of land was generously misinterpreted to retain larger holdings of land. No landholder in record has more than three acres of irrigated land in his land. Thus, falsification of records is a major problem.

Land Acquisition and Displacement

In Maharashtra, the tribals are 9.27 per cent of the population. But among those displaced persons, the tribals were about 27 per cent. In 1979, Maharashtra had the largest number of large dams in the country. 631 dams were either completed or are in the process of being completed. This started a movement against dispossession of land by the local tribal people. These tribals, finding no satisfactory rehabilitation package, took recourse to the Naxalism. Five rehabilitation schemes are there on papers but these are meant for persons who can take advantage of these schemes. Illiterate and simple tribals cannot perhaps, take proper advantage of these schemes. As a result, they are denied their rights. After having lost their agricultural land and home, they have nowhere to go except to join the Naxalite outfits. Thus, the resettlement and rehabilitation work under land acquisition schemes by the government should be given similar priority as land acquisition. Land should be handed over only after the resettlement issues are decided and finalised in the field and not only on papers. This is a very strong dictum for the present day regulatory administration but the government has to choose whether they want to deliver fruits of development only to a few and leave the affected persons in lurch compelling them to join violent/armed outfits. On the other hand, the Press, NGOs and armed groups are now equally vocal and publicity prone to ballooning these adverse effects of any development project. Thus, more caution and proactive action is required on the part of the government as a whole.

Co-operative Farming

There is a proactive experiment going in Pune successfully for many years on the State farm under the Maharashtra State Farming Development Corporation. The land is owned by the individual cultivators but arrangement is made for cultivation through modern implements and inputs collectively. The marketing is also done on cooperative basis. Thus, it is the ideal system of cooperative farming keeping individual ownership intact.

Conclusion

Though the incidents of Naxal violence is increasing in prosperous State of Maharashtra, yet everything is not lost. Maharashtra has lot of resources of fund and personnel. The political will and administrative will are required to be made operational. It seems that in its march towards industrialisation, Maharashtra is forgetting its poor people who feed big cities and big towns. Time is ripe to take a re-look at the implementation of land reform measures along with making minor legislative amendments here and there. The revenue administration is to be given top priority, which was given during seventies. If the development schemes are not implemented or made operational, the land acquired should be returned to the tribals or at least unused or excess land should be returned to them. Panchayat bodies are to be geared up and they should be co-opted in the process of land distribution and even in recording of sharecroppers. The tribals and poor cultivators in Vidarbha and Marathwada regions should be given institutional finance i.e. bank loan for cultivation on concessional rates so that they do not have to commit suicide. Large number of suicides by farmers speaks poorly of the performance of land reforms in the State. Let this blot be removed and Maharashtra should lead in the field of Land Reforms as in the past.

19
Purchase and Distribution of Land

Increase of productivity is the ultimate aim of the land reforms. It was debated by some economists that the minimum farm size should always be there to ensure due productivity of land. The minimum size was estimated up to two ha (5-6 acres approx). On this premise green revolution was launched. But the green revolution turned red in the bastion state of green revolution i.e. Punjab. There was terrorist violence and large scale migration to foreign countries from Punjab. One of the reasons of terrorist violence in eighties was uneven distribution of land and wealth in Punjab.

According to Professor S Swaminathan, only 10 million hectare of land is sufficient for production of 100 million tons of foodgrains in the country, but the country will never be able to invest even in fertilizers at par with advanced countries. What will 70% masses do in villages who are dependent on agriculture and know only how to cultivate land?

The Indian economy has not yet reached the stage to provide them employment. At present, there is a lot of disguised unemployment. The rural folk is employed only to about 30% of their capacity. Therefore, the economic liberalization should not create more unemployment and disguised unemployment in rural areas which will ultimately result into violence destroying all the palaces, malls, structures and buildings.erected by the fast running Indian economy. At present, upsurge of the Naxalism is one of the offshoots of inequitable growth in rural India. Similarly, the animal resource is available in plenty in rural India which can not be otherwise employed by the modern economy. What will bullocks do if there is no work available in rural India for them?

The recent study, by the Food and Agricultural Organization of the United Nations, has found that small land holdings given by Government is creating confidence in rural masses.

"In the later phases of the land reform, the administrators began allocating the vested land in smaller parcels. Given the fact that large numbers of landless are owning even a very small parcel of land, this implementation policy made good sense".

"Most interviewees who commented on the relative effectiveness of the land redistribution stated that those who had received agricultural land had realized significant livelihood improvements as a result. There were, however, some exceptions. One farmer(who had not himself received land) reported that households in his village who had received land had not realized significant benefits because they lacked implements and thus were not able to put the land to good use. The same farmer claimed that some of those beneficiaries had mortgaged their land away to larger farmers. A farmer in another village who had received vested land reported that while the former owner had produced three crops per year, he was only able to produce one crop per year. Two farmers interviewed had received homestead plots. The homestead plots allocated were extremely small, typically 0.04 acres (about 1700 square feet) or less. Even in such tiny plots, we observed that the farmers were growing vegetable or had planted fruit trees for household consumption". (Rural Development Institutes, Washington, USA).

Under 'Green revolution', the contribution of human labour was reduced to about 11% so also of animal labour to 11% (approx). Is required credit available for the poor in rural India like in green revolution? On the other hand, according to a Chinese proverb, the more number of times a farmer visits his field, more will be the production. The small landholder or share-cropper has nothing else to do. He will certainly visit his field more number of times irrespective of the fact that his landholding is very small. Similar experimentation in Bangladesh has met with grand success where three stage cultivation is being undertaken on small plots of land.

The theory of minimum economic holding size has been exploded through experimentation and practical experiences. In the estimates of economic size holding, the major component of agricultural production is human labour ranging from 25% to 30% and animal labour or mechanical implements from 50% to 30%.

Surplus land is not available to satisfy the land hunger of ever growing landless population in rural India. Land is the most precious asset of a villager and is his identity. Land as a resource, can not be extended like rubber. The present political environment is not ripe to lower down further ceiling limit in rural India as middle class has asserted itself and is hankering for more goods and services further at par with its counterparts in the developed world. In the present scenario, no government can run being on warpath with the middle class.

Government of West Bengal has come out with solution. Where there is no surplus Government land available and there are people at the brink of starvation i.e. much below the poverty line, the Government will go for purchase of land from the willing land owners and distribute the purchased land to the landless and the poorest mainly tribals, scheduled castes and dalits. The scheme is summarized below;

Name of the Scheme: Chas-O-Basobaser Bhumidan Prakalpa (Cultivation & Homestead Land Donation Scheme).

Objective of the Scheme:

(i) Economic development through agriculture and rehabilitation of landless and homeless persons of rural areas by distributing agricultural land to them after purchasing the same from intending raiyats.

(ii) Providing inputs of all other line-departments for other developmental schemes, like construction of houses under the Indira Avas Yojana, formation of Self Help Groups to take up other economic activities with the help of DRDC and Banks, etc.

(iii) Providing logistic support and basic services in the compact block within the land to be settled to the group of beneficiaries by constructing road, supply of drinking water, electricity, community toilets, etc. under different rural development schemes.

Manner of Implementation

(i) The scheme was introduced in the year 2005-06. Under this scheme, after giving wide publicity, agricultural land are purchased at the market price from the intending raiyats for distribution of the same to the landless and homeless persons.

(ii) Locations of land are selected in the vicinity where the prospective beneficiaries are residing.

(iii) Purchasing of land is made through registered instrument in favour of Government as per existing norms.

(iv) A beneficiary is allotted more or less 16 decimal of land on permanent basis by executing deed of settlement. No premium is charged for such settlement.

(v) There is a block level committee in each block of this State under the chairmanship of the Sabhapati of the Panchayat Samity. Other members are block development officer, agriculture development officer, Karmadhakshya of Bon-O-Bhumi Sthayee Samity of Panchayat Samity, additional district sub registrar and block land and land officer (Convenor member). The role of the block level committee for implementation of the scheme properly is to identify the eligible beneficiaries, to assess the requirement of land, to settle the purchase of land, and to settle the distribution of land to their approved beneficiaries

(vi) Funds are placed with the district magistrates for disbursement towards cost of land.

Achievement of the Scheme

Year	Fund allotted	Fund utilised	Land purchased	Land distributed	No. of beneficiaries
2005-06 & 2006-07	1000 lakh	72.20 lakh	80.70 acres	80.70 acres	193

During 2007-08 and afterwards, the funds are being utilized and the scheme is in operation in full swing.

Problems

(i) Normally suitable lands are not available. The lands which are available generally have some encumbrances like sharecroppers etc. Land with sharecroppers are not allowed to be purchased under the scheme.

(ii) Beneficiaries fail to cultivate the land properly which were allotted to them but is very far from their residence.

(iii) Agricultural land cannot be used for residential purposes.

(iv) After offering their land some landowners withdraw their offers. This creates lot of complications.

(v) The offer rate and market rate of lands may differ considerably.

Lessons

Block level committees should be strengthened and they must expedite their activities and involve local farmers, societies or organizations if any, for proper selection of land Mostly, the beneficiaries should be selected and then lands should be identified because the people in villages do not want to move far away from their present abode or habitation. This is applicable in all rural development schemes. This is being followed as one of the important guidelines in the Scheme.

Conclusion

This is one of the unique schemes undertaken by the Government of West Bengal in the country towards land reforms.

I am sure that the other states will follow this scheme and Government of India will come in a big way for financial assistance by providing cent per cent grant under the scheme because the land reforms and revenue sector generally are undertaken as non-plan scheme by state governments and such a scheme can only be taken under the planned budget.

Secondly, the state governments are starved of the funds. Therefore, it is with the help of Government of India that such a scheme can take off. West Bengal has always been spearheading the movement of land reforms in the country. This is one of the steps of Government of West Bengal. Even Orissa ex Chief Minister, Biju Patnaik, while inaugurating the seminar on "Poverty elimination in rural development" has said "Orissa should follow West Bengal in implementing land reforms to achieve substantial increase in agriculture production and productivity. The West Bengal Government's recording the rights of sharecroppers on the tenanted lands had helped them in availing of bank credit for investment on land under cultivation. This, in turn, had helped them increase agricultural production by a phenomenal 70 per cent in recent years".

20

Streamlining Revenue Administration for Land Reforms

The implementation of land reforms is done by the oldest government department popularly known as the revenue department. The department is very popular with the countrymen specially with the rural folk as this is the department which is the maker and custodian of land records in the country and has stood with the people in times of needs like drought, flood or other natural calamities. Its key functionary is the collector of the district who is also incharge of law and order in the district.

Traditionally and historically, none has ventured to disturb the hegemony of this institution. On the other hand, there are bouquet of praises from all quarters including foreign researchers and international agencies how the district administration in India operates successfully with the most limited resources at its command by any national or international standard.

The revenue department in a state is headed by the principal secretary or chairman, board of revenue, whosoever is senior. In UP, chairman, board of revenue, is in charge of revenue administration whereas principal secretary does the policy making job. In states like Madhya Pradesh, Rajasthan and few others board of revenue hears and disposes of revenue appeals and revisions before cases go to the High Court. Below the state level apex structure, there is divisional level structure where commissioner of a division consisting of four or five districts is the head. Under the commissioner, is the district collector. Then, there are subdivisional level officers known as SDO and then tahsil or block level officer known by different designations—like tahsildar or block land and land reforms officer. Below the block level, there are revenue inspectors/kanungo consisting of two or three villages. In each village or revenue mauza more, there is patwari, lekhpal, talathi—who keeps the village land record, keeps on updating it according to the system of the state. A talathi is basically an Amin or a technical person who is expert in land measurement and keeping of land records. A revenue inspector above him is also helped by an Amin who is an exclusive survey man.

There are two systems of revenue administration. One is the revenue machinery which functions vertically and is in charge of records as well as management. There is a second system in West Bengal where there is a separate machinery to update and maintain the records periodically and the other agency is for management purpose which records changes in land records by way of disposal of mutation and conversion petitions. In West Bengal, these two agencies have also been merged but at the district level, one post of ADM is kept as district land and land reforms officer who is exclusively for land reform purposes under collector. As collector is one of the busiest functionaries in the country, DL&LRO does all the land reform work on his behalf without formal delegation from the collector. As a result, land reform work does not suffer. But due to merger of survey and settlement and management wing, maintenance and updation of land records work has suffered a lot because collector utilizes them for multifarious jobs at hand which are of emergent in nature. Therefore, there is a case to separate the two wings. If two wings i.e. settlement and management wing cannot be separated, at least employees engaged in settlement work should be exclusive from the firefighting jobs of the collector with a very strict and clear order from the government to implement the same in the field. They shall not be engaged in protocol, land acquisition, elections and other sundry odd works of district magistrate. Apart from arms licensing, maintenance of food and supplies, treasury, the district magistrate is the chief development officer who looks after development works mainly rural development like the Prime Minister Rozgar Yojna, NREGA [National Rural Employment Guarantee Act], Indira Awas Yojna, etc.

Problems faced and solutions suggested

1. As collector is overall in charge of the revenue administration, he engages the revenue machinery in all his odd jobs. For instance, in Uttar Pradesh, revenue administration is mainly busy in protocol duties and VIP matters, revenue administration of Bihar and Rajasthan are busy in attending to land matters of the landed politically powerful persons. In Madhya Pradesh, the revenue administration at one time was doing its real work of measurement of land and giving over possession to the patta holders, but now the machinery has become awfully busy in demarcation of disputed plots and attending to earmarking lands for industries, urban settlement etc. In Punjab and Haryana, the revenue machinery is busy in mutations and conversions apart from land acquisition. In Orissa, the land revenue administration is busy in settling land disputes projected by NGOs and displaced persons due to land acquisition. In south, the land revenue administration of Karnataka and Tamilnadu are doing their original jobs and are trying to modernize the system. In Andhra Pradesh, the Naxalites keep land revenue administration busy in attending to law and order related land problems yet land records machinery is doing its job independently and successfully. In Gujarat, Maharasthra and West Bengal, land revenue administration is attending to the needs of industrialization of the states. Thus, the main focus of land revenue administration is different in different states. There is a separate land acquisition wing under the collector. That wing only should do land acquisition. It should be strengthened as per needs. The survey and settlement machinery should be left for update of land records, maintenance of land records and recording of sharecroppers etc. Distribution of government vested land should be handled by the management wing of land revenue machinery because it involves everybody.

2. The total strength of land revenue administration has not improved with the passage of time and increase of population.

As there is continuous fragmentation of plots, more personnel are required by the land revenue wing because each owner is to be recorded separately in khatian and record-of-rights [Khasra] is to be given to him separately. As a result, no state government ventures into the thorough revision of record-of-rights, which will take 10 to 20 years if continuous work is done. Suppose, required personnel are recruited for survey and settlement work at one go, then where will they go after completion of operation? Therefore, what is being done in the name of update of records is very little. For example, Bihar has less than half the number of staff and officers than West Bengal. Due to poor financial position of majority of state governments including Bihar, Orissa, Assam, Punjab, U.P., the central funds for update or computerization of land records are either not utilized or are diverted. Government of India adopted one central scheme known as "centrally sponsored scheme" of strengthening of revenue administration and updating of land records [SRA&ULR] in 1987-88 on 50:50 sharing basis between the Centre and the States. The main objectives of the scheme were:

(i) Strengthening survey and settlement organizations for early completion and preparation of land records in areas where this work is yet to be completed.

(ii) Setting up survey and settlement organizations especially in the north-east, where no land records exist.

(iii) Imparting pre-service and in-service training to revenue, survey and settlement staff and strengthening training infrastructure for this purpose.

(iv) Providing facilities for modernization of survey and settlement operations, printing survey maps, reports and documents and storage, copying and updating of land and crop records using, among other things, latest science and technology inputs.

(v) Strengthening revenue machinery at the village and immediate supervisory levels on a selective basis to make the workload of functionaries manageable.

Under the scheme, states and UTs have been given assistance for purchase of modern survey equipments like Global Positioning Systems (GPS), EDM, total stations, theodolites, work stations, carrying out aerial surveys, office equipments like photocopiers, laminating machines binding machines and basic facilities to improve work efficiency at lower levels of revenue administration, construction of record rooms for proper storage of land records, construction of office-cum-residence for patwaries and construction, repair and renovation of training institutes and equipment for training.

Table 20.1: Release of funds during first four years of Xth Plan

Year	Funds released [Rs. in crore]
2002-03	20.73
2003-04	24.21
2004-05	19.43
2005-06	39.49
Total	**103.86**

Thus, the allocation of fund for delivery system of land reforms is minimum as compared to other sectors. How can then the results be expected higher?

For further improvement, a scheme titled NLRMP (National Land Resources Management Programme) has been adopted by the Central Government. For every ill in the administration, there is only one pill available with the higher echelons of administration that is computerization. This is also going to be implemented to update land records irrespective of the fact that the land revenue machinery is farthest from the computer as they are deep rooted in the village. Secondly, computer cannot *suo motu* update a record. If garbage is fed in the computer, garbage will come out of it. But computerization can certainly help in current and future work of updating of land records.

The NLRMP will, *inter alia,* focus on citizen services like computerized Records-of-Rights (RoRs) with maps; web-based "anytime-anywhere" access to land data; services through facilitation centers in tehsils and other places; speedy and efficient property registration; automatic initiation of mutation notices; land passbooks - smart cards with all land information including charges and encumbrances; facilitated access to land-based credit/ cooperative banks, etc. It envisages creation of core GIS with cadastral layer for the entire country, 100 per cent digitization of cadastral maps, integration of textual and spatial data, updating of land records using modern technology (aerial photogrammetry, DGPS, ETS), National and State Land Data Banks with specific plot IDs and details, use of uniform land data codes with Indian language script computing, integration with National Spatial Data Base (NSDB) and National Natural Resources Management System (NNRMS), full training and capacity building of the functionaries and National and state missions for effective implementation.

However, in piecemeal survey work will have to be undertaken by all states, which is long overdue. There is no escape from it as far as old records are concerned. Advance administrative set-up will have to be drawn up with investment jointly by the Centre and the states. The survey trained personnel are not available in the market, therefore, the governments will have to recruit from the open market. Even setting up of survey institutes are to be promoted. Then through computerization, current and future revisions in record-of-rights will be duly incorporated without disturbing the record of a village or mouza.

3. The land revenue minister is not generally a senior minister in the state cabinet. He cannot ensure his voice being

heard at the highest policy-making body. If his secretary or principal secretary put some unorthodox suggestions to implement land reforms, the vested interests at once work against him and get him removed. The chief minister is generally surrounded by the industry lobby and is pleased to listen how the industries are developing in his State on papers. The media is very much averse to cover land reform field. In fact, one in hundred in media knows a b c of the land reform. In such a situation, land reform becomes the last priority of the state government and the first casualty in the present run of government. The state government does not like to disturb the status quo in the rural areas, which may prove to be explosive. As a result, the portfolio of land revenue minister may be blown away. None is interested to disturb the status quo. Everybody criticizes yet everyone likes to behave like a bureaucrat in India. Nobody likes to take the responsibility for backlash by the land owning class including middle class who are quite vocal adequately supported by the media. Thus, firefighting goes on. If there are incidents of Naxalite violence, police tackles them and everybody forgets until a fresh incident worth noting occurs. Thus, the bureaucratic country is happy indulging in fire fighting. Even the land revenue commissioner is happy to shirk his responsibility by saying that law and order is in the police domain. They can do some tangible or proactive work of land reform only when peace is restored in the area. And this peace bird eludes everybody. As a result, land revenue department sits idle.

However, everything is not lost in India. There are some nationalist and patriotic officers and officials who work and continue working for the rural poor without any appreciation from their bosses because of their self-commitment and mental make-up. These reform personnel or change-agents are present in administration in a sizeable number who also keep on suffering for their genuine causes and convictions for the poor. Pen is in their support and will continue bleeding for them. It is hoped that their lone battle will bring good sense among the rest of bureaucracy and the political elite who at least will allow them to work impartially and objectively without unnecessary and unwanted interference from the top. The blessing eyes of the dumb majority of the dalits and the adivasis are enough sources of inspiration, which will keep them and their families happy in the long run because they are serving the 'daridranarayana' of Gandhiji. New technologies can also be employed like aerial survey for preparation of rough photo record of the plots of land and then K-B, attestation, etc. can follow.

If the state governments are serious, they should appoint men of calibre as land revenue minister who has the knowlege of the job and is known for his work by the people in the field. The revenue minister should be such a senior person who cannot be cowed down easily by his cabinet colleagues or the chief minister. This minister will be able to protect his reform oriented secretary or officers and staff of the department. Otherwise the opponent side is so apt in making complaints couched in a logical language that the revenue minister or chief minister will be taken by their rhetoric and will punish his reform oriented personnel who will then be demoralized and frustrated and leave the initiatives. It does not mean that all is well with the land revenue machinery. It is already branded corrupt. But abolition of posts of patwaris could not solve the problem. Someone at the lowest level has to keep the land records which is the basic duty of every government so that two raiyats or owners or occupiers or claimants of one piece of land do not fight and disturb public peace and tranquility. Time is ripe to add more personnel to the revenue department and make it an efficient vehicle of land reforms in the interest of the poor and the downtrodden. The same machinery when strengthened will take care of updation and maintenance of land records in urban areas including metropolitan towns. There are common service centers in gram panchayat level which will keep the latest records-of-rights on computer. Any person/owner can verify his R-o-R there.

If political interference is reduced, motivated and efficient officers will opt for posting in the revenue department because this is basically their parent department. It has been at present made so unattractive and dull that none likes to shoulder the responsibility. If the surplus land of the department is to be allotted among the industries, real estate people or among the service organizations, the chief secretary of the State will jump in and will become the chairman of the allotment committee. Anyhow, if chief secretary does not have the time, he will entrust this work to his most entrusted lieutenant as per instruction of chief minister so that the chief minister can control fruits of land department. If above could not be done through one window clearance, industry department will control the surplus land of the revenue department. The revenue department will continue to make records and handover the surplus land to somebody else. In case of land acquisition, the land revenue department cannot question the real requirement of industry or service or commercial sector, which is forwarded to him by the concerned department in a balloon form. All hell will let loose on it and the revenue department will ultimately lay down arms. Is th': the environment, in which the land reforms can be implemented?

Implementation of land reforms requires strong political will which will permeate up to the last ladder of the revenue administration. The land revenue minister should be a person of high status who can say 'No' to anybody. He is the custodian, protector and leader of all the patta-holders and sharecroppers (tenants) in the State and he should discharge this role in a true spirit and with devotion to the teeming millions of India who hardly have their spokesman left.

Conclusion

It is a fact that there are insurmountable difficulties in gearing up the revenue administration in the country. Firstly, because the subject is exclusively with the state government and secondly, because it requires huge investment which may not be forthcoming easily due to present financial position of most of the states. Therefore, the Central Government should immediately intervene and grant the required financial assistance otherwise the Central Government will have to spend many more times funds on containing Naxalite violence in rural areas or other problems of unrest including divisive flare-ups.

Without gearing up delivery agency i.e. the revenue department, the discussion about implementation of land reforms will be like beating the drums behind the bush. It is high time that the revenue department once again realizes its role of sheat-anchor in the country and plays it well which it had done after the independence in nineteen fifties and sixties and in West Bengal in nineteen eighties and nineties. If reform is seriously intended, the traditional machinery is required to be thoroughly geared up or given a parallel new support of personnel and technology which will meet the new challenge properly.

It is hoped that there will be requisite political will at the highest level which will generate required administrative will. As a result, Naxalite like agitations will end soon.

Index

Abolition of
  Zamindari, 28
  Zamindari, Jagirs, Inams, 29
Acquisition—Agricultual
  Labourers Act, 64
Adhikar Abhiyan, 126
Adivasis, 22, 150
Adivasi Tendu Leaf Gatherers, 22
Administration, 17, 20, 51, 56, 58, 63, 85, 120, 121, 124, 189, 197, 201
  District, 93, 197
Affected Districts, 111
  Bankura, 111
  Purulia, 111
  West Medinapur, 111
Agrarian
  Reforms, 17, 28, 183
  Struggle, 88
Agricultural
  Cooperatives, 127
  Economy, Diversification of, 28
  Export Zone, 179
  Labour, 25, 70, 88
  Labourers, 36, 37, 55, 116, 117
Alienation, 124
Alleviating Rural Poverty, 27
Andhra Pradesh, 22, 63, 65, 66, 71, 86, 95, 102, 146
  Land Reform Act, 165
  Land Reforms in-, 157-172
  Land Reforms Ceiling on Agricultural Holding, 160
  Scheduled Areas Land Transfer Regulations, 159
Anti-Naxalite Cell, 101
Armed
  Maoist Cadre, 94
  Revolution, 16
Arms and Ammunition, 86
Army of Landless—, 23
Assam, 71
Author,
  Addl District Magistrate (Land Reforms), 59
  Addl District Magistrate (Murshidabad), 59
  Addl District Magistrate (Purulia), 59
  Director of Land Records and Surveys, 59
  District Magistrate and Collector, Coochbehar District, 59
  Organized Patta Distribution Camps, 59
  Principal Secy and Land Reforms Commissioner, 59

Automation—Registration Procedure, 80
Ayub Khan, Dictator of Pakistan, 26

Backward
  District Initiatives (BDI), 97
  Regions Grant Fund (BRGF), 98
Baiga Tribe, 89
Bandyopadhyaya, D, 52, 101
  Commission, 147
Bangladesh, 16, 115
Barga Operation, 21, 107
Bargadars, 50, 52, 54, 55, 56, 58, 62, 64, 138
  Cultivators, 60
Bastar
  And Godchiroli, 127
  Region, 97
Benamdari, 142
Benami, 65
  Lands, 52, 57, 62, 85
  Names, 142
  Transactions, 138
  Transactions Act, 65
  Transfers, 120, 138
Bhoodan
  Act Implementation, 31
  Land, 13, 15, 28, 132
    Distribution of-, 141
Bhumi Swamis, 126
Bhumijivi Sangh, 60
Bhumkal, Rebellion against British, 127
Bihar, 17, 21, 63, 65, 96, 137
  Land Ceiling Act, 146
  Land Reforms in-, 141-148
  Scheduled Caste Population, 142
Bihar—Uttar Pradesh, 200
Block Development Officer (BDO), 51
Block Land and Land Reforms Officer (BLLRO), 51
Board of Revenues, 54
Bombay Tenancy and Agricultural Land Act, 185
BPL, 102, 111
  Category, 174, 175
  Landless, 64
Bureaucrats, 52

Cabinet Committee on Security (CCS), 99
Capitalism, 28
Ceasefire, 102
Ceiling, 115, 139
  Act (Govt. of India) 1974, 70
  Acts, 38
  In Agricultural Land Holdings, 158
  Laws, 30, 120, 162
  Legislation, 120
  Limits, 46
  Limits in Various States, 45
  On land Holdings, 28, 46
  Surplus Land, 141
Central
  Organizing Committee, 19
  Para Military Forces, 96
  Recruitment, 96
Central Committees in-, (CCI), 19

Bihar, 19
Chhattisgarh, 19
Jharkhand, 19
Madhya Pradesh, 19
Maharashtra, 19
Orissa, 19
Charitable Organizations, 56
Chas-O-Basobaser Bhumidan Prakalpa, 193
Objectives, 193
Chatterjee, Kanai, 20, 83
Chauhan, Shiv Raj, CM-MP, 132
Chauri (Bhojpur), 18
Chhattisgarh, 63, 84, 96, 97, 124, 128, 132
And Jharkhand, 88, 89
Mukti Morcha, 123
Population, 123
Chief Ministers Conf on Ceiling of Agricultural Holdings, 30
China, 16
Choudhury, Binoy Krishna, 52
Civil
Jurisprudence, 46
Liberties Groups, 94
Colombia, 26
Committees of Beneficiaries, 31
Common
Property Resources (CPR), 126
Service Centre (CSC), 169
Communist Party of India (M), 16
Computerization of Land Records in-, (CLR), 72
Scheme, 72, 73, 80
Gandhinagar (Gujarat), 72
Mayurbhanj, (Orissa), 72
Morena (MP), 72
Rangareddy (AP), 72
Singhbhum (Bihar), 72
Sonitpur (Assam), 72
State-wise Achievements, 74-77
Wardha (Maharashtra), 72
Comrade Mao, 16, 86
Contract Farming, 179
Cooperative
Farming, 33, 35, 37, 41, 63, 190
Society(ies), 29, 63, 124, 154
CPI (Maoist), 18, 21, 50, 56, 66, 107, 166
CPI (M-L People's War), 19
CPI (ML), 16, 84
CPML-PWG, 20
CPM-PWG, 20
Crash Programme of Operation Barga, 54
Criminal Justice, 20
Crop Finance, 107
Crop-Credit Finances, 39
Cultural Administration, 93

Dalits
and Adivasis, 90
and Tribals, 150
Panther Agitators, 17
Dandakaranya 'Guerrilla Zone', 127
Daridranarayan of Gandhiji, 204
Darjeeling, 63
Debt Relief Regulations, 160
Densely Populated States, (DPS), 69
Kerala, 69
West Bengal, 69

Devasthan, 183
Development of Public Land, 27
Digitization of Maps, 146
Direct Targets of Violence, 15
Directive Principles of State Policy, 27
Distribution of Land, 186
District
  Administration, 93
  Aurangabad, 17
  Bastar, 18, 125, 129
  Bhojpur and Patna, 17
  Bijapur, 97
  Chandrapur (Maharashtra), 129
  Dantewada, 97, 125
  Gaya, 17
  Gwalior and Morena, 132
  Jabalpur, 129
  Kalahandi, 155
  Kankar, 125
  Karnataka and TN, 21
  Mirzapur, 118, 121
  Monghyr, 17
  Nalgonda, 165
  Purulia, 55
  Rohtas, 17
  Singhbum (Jharkhand), 17
  Sonbhadra, 118
Divisional Committees, 83

East
  Bengal State Acquisition and Tenancy Act, 1950, 26
  Pakistan (now Bangladesh), 26
Economic
  And Social Development, Barriers for-, 26
  Development, 193
  Growth, 28
  Liberalization, 191
  System, 27
Economy, 28
  Indian, 191
  Labour Intensive, 61
  Modern, 192
  Rural, 25, 28
Egalitarian
  Social Structure, 28
  Society, 52, 118
Egypt, 33
Egypt Patterns, 47
Ekta Parishad, NGO, 132, 149
Election Commission, 18
Elections, 50
Electronic Total Stations (ETS), 80
Empowered Group of Ministers (EGOM), 100
Erstwhile Districts of MP, (EDOM), 123
  Bastar, 123
  Bilaspur, 123
  Durg, 123
  Raigarh, 123
  Raipur, 123
  Rajnandgaon, 123
  Sarguja, 123
Extortion from Business—Govt. Officers, 20
Extremist Outfits, 91
Ex-Zamindars of-, (EZ), 142
  Darbhanga, 142

Dumraon, 142
Hathwa, 142
Ramgarh, 142

Farming Cooperative Societies, 47
Farzi Parivar Register, 120
Festivals and Rituals, 38
Finance Commission (12th), 112
Financial Institutions, 78
Fire Fighting Mechanism, 91
Food and Agriculture Organization (UNO), 47, 48, 110, 192
Forced Labour (Begari), 22
Forest
Areas of -, (FA), 22
Andhra Pradesh, 22
Chhatisgarh, 22
Vidarbha Region of Maharashtra, 22
Cases, 132
Conservation Act, 1980, 131
Forests of-, 22
Warangal, 22
West Godavari, 22
Fundamental Rights, 28, 43

Gandhi, Smt. Indira, 17
General Elections, 16
Giridih (Bihar), 18
Global Positioning System (GPS), 79, 80, 201
Goa, 71
Golakhnath Case, 43
Gond and Baiga, 130, 131
Government Wasteland, Distribution of-, 142
Govt. Surplus Land in UP, Distribution of-, 115-121
Gram
Nyayalayas, 34
Panchayat, 52, 64
Sabha, 135
Green Revolution, 191
Greyhounds, 96
Guerrilla Formations, 84
Guerrilla Zone, 84

Heart Land States (Naxalites), (HLS), 20
Andhra Pradesh, 20
Bihar, 20
Chhattisgarh, 20
Madhya Pradesh, 20
Maharashtra, 20
West Bengal, 20

IKP Project, 166
Implementation of Land Reforms, 137
Indebtedness and Drinking, 38
Indian
Economy, 191
Forest Act, 132
People's Front (IPF), 18
Reserve Battalions, 96
Society, 150
Indira Avas Yojna (IAY), 64, 176, 193
Infrastructure, 137
Institutional Financing, 63, 173
Integrated
Rural Development Program, (IRDP), 35, 55, 117
Tribal Development Program (ITDP), 32, 35, 55, 117, 134
Intelligence Bureau, Directorate, 91

Inter-Ministerial Group (IMG), 99, 100
Internal Security, 100
Irrigational Facilities, 39

Jammu and Kashmir, 71, 89
Jan Adalats, 20
Janta Sarkar, 127
Jawahar Rozgar Yojna, (JRY), 30, 32, 35, 117
Jharkhand (State), 20, 63, 65, 84, 89, 96, 137, 141, 142
  Land Classification, 139
  Land Reforms in-, 137
Joint
  Forest Management (JFM), 130
  Land Reforms Commissioner, 17
Judiciary, 21
Junior Land Reforms Officer (JLRO), 56

Kalahandi, 149
Karnataka, 66, 84, 146
  And West Bengal, 168
  Land Tribunal, 176
  Technology Giant, 173
Kashipur, 149
Kerala, 64
Khanapuri Bujharat (KB), 55
Khand Samiti, 117
Kidnapping, 20
Kilavemani (Tamil Nadu), 17
Kisan Sabha, 32, 33
Kitchen Garden Scheme, 103
Kondapalli Seetharamaiah (KS), Naxalite Leader from AP, 19
Krishak
  Organization, 41
  Sabha, 50, 66
Kurmi, Backward Caste, 17

Labour Generating Schemes, 63
Land
  Acquisition, 89, 187
  Alienation, 123
  Ceiling Acts, 123
  Ceiling in Orissa, 154
  Ceiling Programme, 163
  Distribution, 110
    In Asian Region (LDAR), 26
      China, 26
      India, 26
      Japan, 26
      Karnataka, 175
      South Korea, 26
      Taiwan, 26
    Programme, 58
    Scheme, 112
  Identity Cards, 59
  Legislation, 63
  Mines, 84
  Records, 36, 138, 168, 204
    And Surveys, Director of-17
    Computerization (LRC), 71-80
    In Maharashtra, 183-190
    System, Modernization of-28
    Updation in Karnataka, 180
  Reforms, 17, 21, 43-48, 63, 98
    Acts, 29
    And Productivity, 46
    Commissioner, 58
    Committees, 110, 112

Defined, 25-34
Factors Constituting-, 35-42
Implementation of-, 49-68
In Chhattisgarh, 123-128
In Gujarat, 70
In Karnataka, 173-181
In West Bengal, 49, 107-114
Laws, 70
Laws of Orissa and Bihar, 64
Legislation, 158, 176
Litigation, 34
Machinery, 57, 59
Major Objectives, 28
Measures (LRMs), 27, 29, 47, 49, 50, 61, 63, 70, 143, 149
In Tamil Nadu, 70
In West Bengal, 66
People's
Participation, 139
Weaknesses, 187
Programmes, 112
Redistribution of Rights, 25
Revenue Administration, 197, 199
Rules, 52

Land
Revenue Commission, (East Bengal), 26
Rights of Tribals in Orissa, 149-155
Tilting Appellate Tribunal, 170
Tribunals, 34, 69, 70

Landed
Class, 25
Property in India, 27, 28
Landless
Peasantry, 59
Rural poor, 28
Landowners, 84
Lanjigarh, 149
Law and
Administration, 51
Order Problems, 47
Lawful Rights of Bargadars, 62
LBS National Academy of Administration, 175
Left Front
Government, 21, 61, 107
Parties in West Bengal, 50
Rule in West Bengal, 49
Left Parties Allies, 50
Left Wing Extremist (LWE) Group, 20, 143
Legal Aid, 38
System, 124
To Landless, 36
Legal Persecutions, 62
Liberation, 18, 19
Liquidation of Rural Indebtedness, 62
Lok Adalats, 34
Lord Jagannath, 149, 154

Madhya Pradesh, 63, 71, 124, 130, 133, 146, 197, 199
Administration, 126
Land Reform Measures in-, 129
Maharashtra, 65, 96
Agricultural Land Act, 183

State Farming Development Corp., 185, 190
Maintenance of Land Records Act, 1973,
Chhotanagpur Tenancy Act (CNT Act), 147
Major Land Reforms, 50
Majumdar, Charu, Secy. Gen. CPI (M-L), 16, 83, 86
Manipur Land Reform and Land Reform Act, 71
Mao Tse Tung, 16, 86
Mao Zedong, 88
Maoist Communist Centre (MCC), 19, 20, 83, 84
Frontal Organizations, 83
Recruitment, 85
Sources of Income, 87
Strategy, 86
Maoist, 21, 22, 127, 128, 147
New Bases States (MNBS), 93
Delhi, 93
Haryana, 93
Kerala, 93
Punjab, 93
Tamil Nadu, 93
Uttar Pradesh, 93
Uttarakhand, 93
Revolution, 16
Marathwada, (Maharashtra), 17
Marginal Farmers, 17, 108
Mass Media, 95
Massacre in Pipra, 17
Measures of Land Reforms, 47
Mechanized Farming, 61
Mining Projects, 149
Ministry of
Environment and Forest, 98
Home Affairs, 96, 99
Minor Forest Produce (MFP), 135
Modern Economy, 192
Modus Operandi of Naxalites, 97
Money
Lenders, 124
Lending Regulations, 160
Monitoring Mechanism, 98
Movable and Immovable Properties, 84
Mushari in Muzaffarnagar District, 17

National
Agenda (India), 28
Integrations, 26
Land Reforms Council (NLRC), 104
Land Resource Management Programme, (NLRMP), 80, 81, 201, 202
Natural Resources Management System (NNRMS), 81, 202
Rural Employment Guarantee Programme, (NREGP), 30, 35, 55, 117
Spatial Data Base (NSDB), 81, 202
Naxal Affected Districts (NAD), 97
Andhra Pradesh, 97
Bihar, 97
Chhattisgarh, 97
Jharkhand, 97
Madhya Pradesh, 97
Maharashtra, 97

Orissa, 97
Uttar Pradesh, 97
West Bengal, 97
Naxal(s)
Active Areas, (NAA), 16
Bihar, 16
Eastern UP, 16
Jammu and Kashmir, 16
Kerala, 16
North East Area of Andhra Pradesh, 16
Tamil Nadu, 16
Affected States, 96
Force, 88
Group, 86, 98
Organization, 87, 89
Politics, 18, 19
Violence, 93, 96, 190
Weak Operations in-, (NWOP), 16
Assam, 16
Delhi, 16
Gujarat, 16
Himachal Pradesh, 16
Karnataka, 16
Maharashtra, 16
Manipur, 16
Nagaland, 16
Orissa, 16
Punjab, 16
Rajasthan, 16
Western UP, 16
Naxalbari in Darjeeling District (North Bengal-WB), 15, 16, 88
Naxalism, 15-23, 88, 91-114, 126, 129, 137, 176, 191
As Red Terrorism, 18
In Andhra Pradesh, 199
Legacy of-, 17
Movement, 16
Naxalite(s), 16-18, 86, 88, 90, 94, 102, 111, 112, 127-131, 149, 150, 173, 185
Activities, 129
Agitation, 22
Agitation in-, (NA), 67
Andhra Pradesh, 67
Bihar, 67
Chhattisgarh, 67
Jharkhand, 67
Madhya Pradesh, 67
Orissa, 67
Attacks—Dacoity, 84
Claim as Communist Revolutionaries, 16
Group, 92
Ideology, 94, 95
In Bihar, 17
Menace, 94, 97
Movement, 15-23, 88-90, 107
Outfits, 83, 187
Policies to deal with-, 94-95
Problem, 93, 99, 101, 127
Uprising, 92
Violence, 92, 206
Violence in Andhra Pradesh, 157
Neo-Liberalization of Economy, 61
Nepal, 16, 88
New Constituted States in India (NCS), 26
Chhattisgarh from Madhya Pradesh, 26

Jharkhand from Bihar, 26
Uttarakhand from Uttar Pradesh, 26
Niyogi, Comrade Shanker Guha, 123
Non-Governmental Organizations (NGOs), 47, 94, 126, 155, 199
North East States, 63, 65
NREGA (National Rural Employment Guarantee Act), 134, 198
Nyaya Panchayats, 34, 38

Occupancy Rights, 70
In Karnataka, 70
Old Age Pension, 62
Operation
Barga, 50, 52-56, 60, 61, 64, 146
Benefits from, 59
Salient Features of-, 55
Bataider, 116, 118
Orissa, 63, 71, 84, 96, 149
Land Reform Act (ORL), 154

Pakistan, 26
Panchayat
Act, (PESA), 99
Bodies, 21, 109
Extension Act, 168
Functionaries, 58
Samity, 57, 111, 194
Panchayati Raj Institutions (PRIs), 126
Panchayats, 33, 34, 37, 41, 58, 64, 109, 117
Para Military Force, 86, 92
Party Unity (PU), 84
Patnaik, Biju, CM Orissa, 63, 196
Patta Distribution
Camps, 57
Programme, 57
Pattadars, 57, 62-64, 118
Peasant's Organization, 63, 66
Peasants
Committee on Naxalism, 17
Organization, 32, 33, 50, 51, 58
Struggles in-, (PS), 21, 107
Andhra Pradesh, 21, 107
Bihar, 21, 107
Chhattisgarh, 21, 107
Jharkhand, 21, 107
Punjab, 21, 107
West Bengal, 21, 107
People's
Courts, 102
Organizations, (PO), 83
Communist Young League, 83
Farmers Movement Front, 83
Intellectual Organization, 83
Labourers Liberation Organization, 83
Revolutionary Cultural Organization, 83
Revolutionary Farmers Committee, 83
Revolutionary Students League, 83
Women Liberation Association, 83
War Group (PWG), 18, 19, 22, 83, 84, 102

Armed Operations, 19
Personal Cultivation, 31, 45
Peru, 88
Philippines, 26, 88
PM Rozgar Yojna, 30, 32, 35, 103, 198
PM Sarak Rozgar Yojna, 103, 117
Police
  Administration, 23, 127
  And Administration, 143
  Arms Loot, 84
  Organizations, 91
Political Parties, 50, 56, 61, 66
Private Irrigation, 139
Pro-Land Reforms Legislation, 50
Property
  Registration, 80
  Relations, 25
Public Trusts, 70

Rajasthan, 197
Ray, Siddhartha Shankar, 16
Records of Rights, (RoR), 46, 141, 144, 146, 169, 185, 200, 202, 204
Red Terrorism, 90
Redistribution of
  Landed Property, 25
  Lands, 29
Regional
  Committees, 83
  Land Corporation for Bargadars, 61
Rehabilitation and Resettlement,99
Religious and
  Charitable Trusts, 57
  Social Organizations, 46
Restoration of Alienated Tribal Land, 28
Revenue Administration, 199
  System, 198
Revenue Machinery, 143, 199
Revolutionary Struggles, 20
Right of
  Cultivation, 29
  Property, 28, 43
RSVY, (Rashtriya Sam Vikas Yojna), 98
Rural
  Courts, 34
  Development Institute in USA, 47
  Economy, 25, 28
  India, 22, 43, 47, 193
  Sanitation Schemes, 64
  West Bengal, 51, 52

Salwa Judum, 126, 127, 128
Anti-Naxal Movement, 97
Samjukta Kisan Sabha, 66
Samta Judgement, 168
Santhal Parganas, 89
Sanyal, Kanu, 17
Scandal, 17
Scheduled Castes, 150
  Marginal Farmers, 108
  Pattadars, 62
  Population, 129
Scheduled Castes/Tribes, 108, 174, 183
  Community, 70
  Landless BPL Families, 111
  Marginal Farmers, 108
Scheduled Tribe, 70, 109, 132

Population, 129, 149
Tribes (Regulation of Forest Rights), Bill, 98
And Other Traditional Forest Dwellers—Act, (STORFA), 130, 135
Problems, 131
Marginal Farmers, 108
Pattadars, 62
Sector,
Agriculture, 26, 125
Industrial, 28
Self-Help Groups (SHGs), 63, 193
Sen, Amulya, 20, 83
Separatist Agitation, 63
Settlement Operation, 138
Sharecroppers, 29, 30, 49, 50, 61, 61, 62, 64, 69, 123, 138, 143, 154, 177
Patterns, 125
Sharecropping, 115, 116
In UP, 116
System, 61
Shri Jagannathji Religious and Charitable Trust, 151
Sikkim, 71
Small-Medium and Medium Farmers, 108
Social
And Religious Reforms, 36, 38
Conservation, 39
Distortions, (SD), 25
Rise in Crime in Rural India, 25
Suicides by Farmers, 25
Violations, 25
Forestry, 130
Imbalances, 25
Justice, 28
Reforms, 38
Security, 61, 62
Society, Egalitarian, 28
Sonbhadra (UP), 89
Special Zone Committees, 83
Spread of Movement (States), (SM), 16
Andhra Pradesh, 16
Assam, 16
Bihar, 16
Jammu and Kashmir, 16
Orissa, 16
Tamil Nadu, 16
Uttar Pradesh, 16
Srikakulam (Andhra Pradesh), 18, 89
State Land
Corporation for Bargadars, 61
Data Bank (SLDB), 81
State List (Of Subjects), 43
State-wise Pending Cases (In High Courts), 44
Status of Alienation, 132
Strengthening of Revenue Administration, (SRA), 78, 80 200
Main Objectives, 78
Structural
Changes, 54
Reforms, 25
Suicides of Farmers, 67
In Andhra Pradesh, 67
In Vidarbha, 67
Supreme Court, 43-46, 60, 158
Surplus Land, 29, 30, 33, 35, 36, 38, 46, 56, 59, 142, 151

Surplus Land in-, (SL), 123
Basna, 123
Pithora, 123
Sarcipati, 123
Swaminathan, Dr. S, 191

Telengana
Movement, 161
Region of Andhra Pradesh, 84, 158, 161
Tenancy, 30, 32, 35, 109
Act, 163
Ban, 178
Cases, 71
Cultivation/Barga Cultivation, 50
Legislation, 185
Movements, 46
Prohibition Policy in Karnataka, 178
Reforms, 28, 46, 163, 167, 177, 185
Regulations, 178
Rights of Cultivators, 60
Tenure Security, 178
Tenurial and Ownership Rights, 30
Terrorism Defined, 15
Terrorist Organization, 15
Third Party Congress, 18
Tibet, 16
Total Watershed Planning (TWP), 125
Traditional Forest Dwellers, 130
Training
Centres, 86
Of Administrative Personnel, 137
Of Revenue Officers, 162
Of Survey Personnel, 145
Transfer
And Alienation of Agricultural Land, 43
Of Ownership of Land, 29
Of Patta Lands, 58
Of Tribal Land, 134
Tribal(s), 16, 124, 130, 139
Areas 30, 31, 135
Belts of-, (TB), 149
Andhra Pradesh, 149
Chhattisgarh, 149
Jharkhand, 149
Orissa, 149
Community, 147
Land, 39, 124, 132, 136, 167
Alienation, 160, 184
In Andhra Pradesh, 167
Restoration, 132
People, 16
Population, 39
Welfare, 139
Tri-Junction Areas of-, (TJA), 18
Andhra Pradesh, 18
Bihar, 18
Jharkhand, 18
Madhya Pradesh, 18
Orissa, 18
UN (United Nations)
Report, 25, 27
Resolution, 26
United Front Ministry, 16

Updating of Land Records (ULR), 77, 78, 80, 200
  Main Objectives, 78
Uttar Pradesh, 199, 200
  And Bihar, 62
  Imposition of Ceiling on Land Holding Act, 118
  Land Laws, 64
  Land Revenue Act, 64
  Revenue Administration, 115
  Zamindari Abolition Act, 115

Vidarbha Region, 185, 186, 190
Villupuram, 17
Violation of Human Rights, 16
Violence
  Based Communication Processes, 15
  In Belchha, 17
Violent Revolution, 16
Voluntary Organizations, 32, 33

Wakf Inam Grants, 183
Warangal Forest, 102
West
  Godavari, 102
  Medinapur (WB District), 18
West Bengal, (WB), 16, 21, 21, 49, 50, 54, 55, 58, 59, 61, 63-66, 69, 101, 103, 107-114, 115, 118, 138, 143, 142, 146, 149, 166, 179, 195, 196, 199
  Land Reform Act, 50, 53, 54, 56, 57, 140, 170, 171
  Leaders in Land Reforms, 69
  Legislative Assembly, 52
Wynad Jungles (Kerala), 18

Yadavs, 17

Zamindari, 117, 142, 143
  Abolition and Land Reform Act, 121
  System in India and Pakistan, 26
Zamindars, 26, 56